The Wedding Hear  ond

THE WEDDING HEARD 'ROUND THE WORLD

AMERICA'S FIRST GAY MARRIAGE

MICHAEL McCONNELL

WITH

JACK BAKER

AS TOLD TO GAIL LANGER KARWOSKI

• • •

With a New Epilogue

UNIVERSITY OF MINNESOTA PRESS

MINNEAPOLIS • LONDON

Published by the University of Minnesota Press
111 Third Avenue South, Suite 290
Minneapolis, MN 55401-2520
http://www.upress.umn.edu

Library of Congress Cataloging-in-Publication Data
Names: McConnell, Michael. | Baker, Jack.
Title: The wedding heard 'round the world : America's first gay marriage / Michael McConnell, Jack Baker with Gail Langer Karwoski.
Description: Minneapolis : University of Minnesota Press, 2016. | Includes index.
Identifiers: LCCN 2015030115 | ISBN 978-1-5179-1065-5 (pb)
Subjects: LCSH: Same-sex marriage—Minnesota. | Gay rights—Minnesota. | BISAC: SOCIAL SCIENCE / Gay Studies.
Classification: LCC HQ1034.U5 M33 2016 | DDC 306.84/809776—dc23
LC record available at http://lccn.loc.gov/2015030115

Printed in the United States of America on acid-free paper

The University of Minnesota is an equal-opportunity educator and employer.

25 24 23 22 21 20   10 9 8 7 6 5 4 3 2 1

To Mother,
Vera McConnell,
who always told us kids that
we were as good as anyone else.
I've tried to make her proud.

To Jack's maternal grandmother,
Margaret Danek,
who nurtured him from
orphaned child to fine young man.

To our treasured friend,
Cruz Moreno Sanchez,
who first said that Jack and I
were destined for each other.
He was right.

Contents

At our dinner table in Minneapolis, 1970. Photograph by Charlotte Brooks.

Prologue

Jack finishes dinner first and lays his folded napkin on the solid surface of our round oak table. How many times have I seen him do this? This man—my husband for more than forty years—hasn't changed much from the young man I met when I was a college student in Norman, Oklahoma, in the sixties.

I know that everyone sees themselves at the center of their own stage, and every couple feels like they are creating their own universe. But for us, getting married really did set off tremors that ripped through the solid surface of our culture. After our union was announced, we received thousands of letters from around the United States, from Canada and Mexico, from Chile, Argentina, Norway, Israel, and India. The letter writers hailed our wedding as both a model for action and an inspiration for dreams.

Of course, we didn't think of ourselves that way. We were young and in love. We were announcing who we were, pledging to love and honor each other, to uphold our commitment through sickness and health. But we did understand that we were jump-starting social change by tossing a monkey wrench into an antiquated system. Then we stood back, our arms around each other, and waited as the system struggled to reboot.

My husband is Jack Baker. He became the darling of the national media in 1970, the year he was elected the first openly gay university student body president. My name is Michael McConnell. Ours is the world's first gay marriage.

I was in historic Deerfield, Massachusetts, when my friend Terry snapped this shot (top). Jack (bottom) was at the wedding of his best friend from high school. Both photos are circa 1966. Photograph at top by Terry C. Vanderplas.

1

Dancing

.

Jack and I met on October 29, 1966.

We were at a Halloween barn party outside my hometown of Norman, Oklahoma. Kay Fortner owned the barn. (And if you're wondering—yes, Kay is a guy and that really is his name.) He was known for giving extravagant parties where gay guys from the University of Oklahoma (OU) and surrounding areas could socialize.

At the party, my friend Cruz Sanchez, a grad student at OU, grabbed my arm. "Michael, come with me," he said. "There's a guy here that you absolutely must meet. His name is Jack Baker. Trust me, you two are destined for each other."

"Yeah, right," I remember thinking.

Cruz led me through the crowd. As soon as I saw Jack, I perked up. Wow, what a gorgeous guy! He stood about six feet tall, lean body, arms that rippled with muscle. His facial features could have been chiseled onto a Greek statue. The whole package reminded me of Ricky Nelson on the TV show *Ozzie and Harriet*. When he flashed his movie star smile at me, I forgot to breathe.

But as soon as he spoke, I started to get suspicious. Maybe this guy was too good to be true. He didn't sound like a college kid. He talked in the crisp, no-nonsense tones of a businessman, a corporate executive. He had his hair styled in a rigid flattop, with every strand precisely clipped and standing at attention. None of my friends wore their hair like that; most of my friends were college students, and we had casual haircuts that matched our easygoing style of dress. Jack's severe haircut made him look like either a conservative businessman or a soldier.

I started to wonder if Jack was really this guy's name and who he really was. Maybe he was actually a "suit" from the suburbs—a straight man cruising the gay scene in search of casual sex. He wouldn't have been the first man to pull this. I pictured him, an hour before the dance, pecking the pale cheek of some blonde token wife and tucking his 2.5 kids into bed before tooling away from his cookie-cutter suburb in a shiny, late-model car.

I listened for him to slip and give away his secret, but Jack flashed that smile at me again, and my heart started thumping like a puppy's tail. Was this guy ever gorgeous! I forced myself to take a deep breath and consider my options. I fully expected this was going to turn into a one-night stand. After that, I would probably never lay eyes on Jack Baker again. I'm no prude, but I hadn't gone to Kay's dance in search of a casual hookup. Sure, I know there are plenty of guys—gay and straight—who are after meaningless sex, and that's fine. But it's never been me. Ever since I was a kid, I've wanted to find Mr. Right and spend the rest of my life with him.

But this is just a party, I reasoned. What do I have to

lose? So I decided to play along with this Jack Baker. I did remind myself to be careful—don't fall head over heels for this guy. I had recently been through one heartache, and I vowed that I wasn't going to let myself fall hard again—not until I was very, very sure that I could trust the man.

It wasn't easy to be cautious around Jack, though. The way he looked at me made me feel handsome and desirable and delicious. He lavished me with compliments as he traced his finger down the cleft in my chin. Sweeping aside my eyebrow-length bangs, he whispered in my ear, "You have an air of mystery, Michael. You really turn me on."

Jack knew how to dance, and he knew how good he looked on the dance floor. I watched his fluid movements while James Brown's hit song "I Got You" blared through the rafters. When the songs slowed to dreamy, I let myself melt into his strong arms. We were the same height, and our bodies fit together like pieces of a puzzle. It was intoxicating. Careful, Michael, be careful . . .

After the dance, Jack and I went to Joe Clem's house. Joe was a friend of mine, and he had picked up a date at the dance, too. He lived in Norman with his mom, but she was out of town for the weekend so we had the place to ourselves. It was pretty late by the time we got there. We pulled some beers out of the fridge and talked for a few minutes. Then Joe offered Jack and me his mom's room.

The bedroom door closed behind us with a tiny click, and I felt myself tingle with excitement. We didn't turn on the light, but a streetlight filtering through the sheer curtains bathed the room in delicate grays and ambers.

Smiling, Jack reached for me. Up close, I could see the blue of his eyes and the day's growth of beard on his handsome face. His scent made me heady. It felt like a magnet was compelling me toward him. We didn't speak; we both seemed to understand that this was a night to explore and savor. We kissed. Slowly. No need to rush or grab. I slipped out of my shirt and jeans and slid across cool sheets into his warm arms.

Next morning, we said good-bye. I figured this had been a terrific one-night stand and I'd never see Jack Baker again. So I promptly put him out of my head. I got busy with my classes. I had my friends, my life.

The next weekend, I went to another party in Norman, the All Saints Ball. This was a much bigger event, with over two hundred gay guys. Although Jack was there, I didn't spot him in the crowd until the ball became a bust. And at that point, I couldn't have gone over to say hello even if I'd wanted to.

The All Saints Ball turned out to be a memorable evening for everybody who attended. Looking back, I'm convinced that it set the stage for the rest of my life with Jack.

I found out about the All Saints Ball from a mimeographed invitation circulating around the gay bars and through the gay network on campus. Three guys were hosting the ball: Cruz, the friend who had introduced me to Jack at Kay's barn dance; B.J., another of my friends; and David Nance, a casual acquaintance. David was a local businessman. Everybody said he was sometimes bitchy and perhaps a bit lecherous, and that reputation had earned him the campy nickname Nasty Nina. David owned a small candle-making business named Star Brite Studios, and

```
        * ALL SAINTS BALL *

     HALLOWEEN HAS PASSED,
        BUT WE'RE STILL
       IN A HOLIDAY MOOD.
      OUR PARTY WILL BE A
        CRASHING BORE
       WITHOUT YOU . . .


        PLEASE COME!!!!

   Date: Saturday—November 5
    Time: 9:00 pm—'Til
   Place: Star Brite Studios
      501 Columbus Avenue
      Bldg. K13 South Base
       Norman, Oklahoma
```

he rented part of a building on the southern edge of the university's property as his warehouse. Everybody called this area South Base, and that's where the party would be held. David was known for giving great parties, and the All Saints Ball seemed like it would be no exception. All my gay friends said they were going.

I went with a couple of friends, and we arrived around 10 p.m. I've always loved to dance, so I got on the floor and started moving to the beat of sixties music pumped from large speakers set up around the edges of the enormous room. When the familiar lyrics of the Supremes' "Stop! In the Name of Love" blared out, everybody sang along.

Half the ceiling fluorescent lights were turned off, and the room was dimmed like a hotel lounge. Some of David's scented candles flickered on the table of mixers and ice. Most of us had brought our own booze to mix with the punch provided by the hosts. I sipped a drink while I talked with my friends about what they'd been up to. Then I was back on the dance floor, twisting and grooving to "Nowhere to Run" by Martha and the Vandellas. When the sound of "California Dreamin'" by the Mamas and Papas drifted through the air, I wrapped my arms around a cute guy and enjoyed the shivery sensations running up and down my body as we danced cheek to cheek.

It must have been about 1 a.m. when the cops burst in. Four or five of them shoved their way through the crowd. They kept their beefy hands on their holsters just in case somebody made a move. When they reached the front of the room, one of them pulled the plug on the sound system. In the deafening silence, the cop announced the party was over. He ordered us to clear out.

Another cop shouted, "Get out your driver's licenses."

I rolled my eyes. As if it wasn't annoying enough that they were breaking up our party! And for no conceivable reason. We weren't doing anything illegal. The music wasn't disturbing anybody—the warehouse was in an isolated area of campus. Nasty Nina leased the space for his business, so we had the right to be there. We were just a bunch of college kids having fun. But cops love to harass gays—what else is new? To add insult to injury, the bullies were now going to examine our IDs so they could intimidate us with the threat of public exposure.

I stood in line while the cops jotted down my name. It didn't worry me personally because I didn't have anything to hide: I was twenty-four, and I had been out of the closet since I was nineteen. Nobody could intimidate me by telling my parents or professors that I was gay—I had already told everybody I knew.

But some of the guys at the ball were younger than I was, and they were terrified because they were still in the closet. If the cops called their employers or families and reported that they were "homosexuals," it could cause embarrassment. Or worse.

A handful of the partygoers complained when the cops demanded their IDs. As it turned out, Jack's was one of the louder voices. But he wasn't complaining because he was scared—he was angry. He told the cops they had no legal right to see his driver's license. They told him to shut his mouth and get in the squad car. I found out (much later) that he and three or four others spent the next two nights in the county jail. Luckily for Jack, the jail was overcrowded so all the busted partygoers were put into the same cell. It meant they had to sleep on the hard floor since there was only one cot—but it also meant that none of the other inmates would be able to harass them. And that was fortunate because the cops had tried to arrange an unofficial punishment for the "faggots" by circulating a rumor up and down the cell block that some "pretty boys" were in residence.

Luck was on my side, too.

True to form, the cops tracked down my parents' phone number, and one of them called to deliver the "bad news" to Mrs. McConnell that her son Michael was caught attending a gay party.

By that time, my dad had retired and my parents were living in a big ranch-style house on five acres, about six miles outside Norman. It wasn't really a farm—not unless you consider lawn grass a crop. My dad's interest in agriculture was limited to raising bird dogs and quail for hunting.

When the cop called the house, Mother answered. As soon as I got home from class that afternoon, she sat me down in the kitchen.

"Michael, I need to talk to you," she said. "I had this strange phone call today."

I frowned. I figured this had something to do with the All Saints Ball.

"A policeman called," she said. "He asked if I knew that my son was a homosexual."

"What did you tell him?"

"I told him that, yes, of course I knew. And what's that got to do with anything? He said you were at a party that the police raided."

"It was out on South Base, Mother. We weren't doing anything wrong."

"Well, I told the policeman that I know you go to parties, and I assume you were there with your friends." She looked at me, her brows raised. "Now tell me the truth, Michael: You're not hanging around with a bad crowd, are you?"

"Mother, come on, you know my friends. It was mostly a bunch of kids from OU. It was Cruz's party. The cops were just hassling us."

She nodded and touched my arm. "Just so long as you don't get in any trouble." She smiled. "You know we love you, Michael, and we're very proud of you. You just remember what Daddy always says to you kids: We Mc-Connells may not be the richest people in the world, but that doesn't matter. You're just as good as anyone else."

And that was that, as far as my life was concerned. I know I'm lucky that my family has always supported me 100 percent.

In those days, public exposure for a gay man or woman was no joke. People could lose everything—their livelihoods, their standing in the community or the church, their relationship with their family and their friends. That's why it was terrifying for people to admit they were gay. Cruz, for instance, was kicked out of his graduate program after the cops called his department head, and that meant his life was basically derailed. He lost his teaching assistantship. He lost some of the hours he'd already devoted to his doctorate. He ended up moving away from Norman so he could pursue his professional training elsewhere.

When Jack and I discussed—much later—that we'd both been at the "All Saints Bust," we joked about how lucky we had been. He was late to work the following Monday because they wouldn't release him until he went before a judge to request bail. That was ridiculous because Jack certainly wasn't a flight risk—he was an engineer with the Dolese Company, the largest concrete producer in the state, headquartered in Oklahoma City. When court opened at 9 a.m. on Monday and Jack was brought in from the jail cell, he noticed the judge and county prosecutor exchanging smug smiles. Although the judge quickly released Jack on his own recognizance without having to post bail, the whole thing was a big hassle. Besides spending his weekend in jail, Jack had to hire a lawyer (which cost him about fifty bucks) who got the charge dismissed.

Looking back, Jack always says the hassle was a blessing in disguise and well worth what it cost him. It gave him a chance to see the judicial system in action. He was outraged by the cozy way the county officials manipulated the system to harass gays. He had already found out that cops sometimes raided the gay bars around Oklahoma City; those raids had prompted him to write a letter to the editor of the *Oklahoma City Times*. But this time, the harassment was aimed directly at him. They never should have provoked Jack like that. My husband has a mind like a steel trap; he doesn't forget what he learns. Although Jack wasn't able—at that moment in his life—to devote himself to gay rights, the All Saints Bust planted seeds that would take root in the years to come.

Jack also lucked out at his job. Although he didn't get to his desk until noon, nobody noticed because all the managers were in a meeting. And when the cops did call to report that one of their engineers had been picked up at a gay party, the call was routed to the customer relations manager. The manager didn't mention anything to Jack or his boss. Months later, after Jack quit in order to take a higher-paying position at Tinker Air Force Base, the customer relations manager came running out of the building and caught Jack in the parking lot. That's when he finally told Jack about the phone call from the police.

Jack looked at the customer relations manager. "And what did you say to them?"

"That I'd take care of it," the man said and winked.

Jack raised his eyebrows. He had always wondered if this customer relations manager was secretly gay.

Like I said, the All Saints Bust set the stage for the rest of our lives. I'm sure the police never intended to turn us into crusaders or activists by raiding a harmless dance, but that was one of the lasting effects of that evening. The raid demonstrated to us the pointless, hateful persecution of gay men by police and authorities. Neither of us was harmed, physically or emotionally. We always joke that Jack—being part Irish—has the legendary luck of his ancestors. But truthfully, we realize that it's more about our attitude than luck: neither of us has ever caved in to bullies, not to the cops or anybody else. We were both determined to be ourselves in spite of harassment, and that's exactly what we have done. After the All Saints Bust, we knew that someday we would find a way to stand united with other gay men and women and demand to be treated with respect and dignity.

With friends in 1970. Photograph by Charlotte Brooks.

2

Romancing

． ．

After those two eventful weekends, I ran into Jack around
Norman, usually at the homes of mutual friends. As chilly
winds swirled the fallen leaves, we went on a few dates to
movies and campus events. We spent several nights together, and each time I felt totally satisfied. I knew my
attraction to him wasn't just the allure of novelty because
the more we made love, the better it felt.

Gradually, I let down my guard. Jack wasn't at all like
the other gay guys that I knew. He was more serious.
He talked like a grownup, not a kid. But I began to understand that I could trust him. He was exactly who he
seemed to be—not some suit from the suburbs looking for
a quick hookup.

Maybe Jack seemed so different to me because he had
already finished college and had a professional job as an
engineer. When I was a little boy, I used to see engineering students from OU in my dad's barbershop in Norman.
I remember admiring them. They were strong, smart, and
steady. They were always kind to me and courteous to my
dad. I used to dream that I would marry a man like that. It

dawned on me that Jack was just like those engineers I had admired. When I met him, Jack and I were both twenty-four. He knew what he wanted in life just as I did. He was ready for commitment and looking for a steady partner. I began to wonder if I had found the man of my dreams (if only I could convince him to grow his hair out of that ridiculously unfashionable military flattop).

In the opening months of 1967, Jack invited me to a few plays at the Mummers Theater in Oklahoma City. Afterward, I would stay overnight at his apartment in the city rather than drive back to Norman late at night. We began seeing each other regularly, a few times every week. Pretty soon, I was planning my weekends around him.

On one of our early dates, Jack drove directly to my parents' house from his plant. When Mother let him in, she noticed that he had cement dust on his hair. Without a second thought, she offered him a shower and made him feel right at home. Jack flashed his gorgeous smile at her. He was pleasantly surprised by how friendly she was. That was the beginning of a wonderful relationship between them—a relationship that lasted all of her life. In fact, both of my parents liked Jack right away. He was polite and clean-cut. As he became a frequent visitor at our home, Mother took to calling him, jokingly, "my other son."

My parents were kind and wonderful to all of my friends. But there was a reason why they were particularly glad to meet Jack. By the time he and I began to date, my parents had seen me at my lowest point. I had been totally distraught when I moved back home in the fall of 1965, just after a big breakup. I had been with Bob Gaylor, my first lover, for about four years, since I was nineteen years old. I met him when he was a grad student working on his master's degree in library science and I was in my second year of pharmacy school. Bob opened up the world to me. He introduced me to the large, lively, and colorful community of gay men on and around campus. We lived together in Norman and then we moved to Lawrence, Kansas, when Bob took his first job as a librarian at the University of Kansas. When Bob took another job outside Detroit, I moved with him again. But the relationship ended badly. Bob and I wanted different things from life. I adored him, and I wanted a lifelong commitment. He loved me, but he wanted a more casual relationship. I finally realized that he wasn't going to change, and we broke it off. I was crushed.

When I came back home, I was an emotional wreck. I tortured myself with doubts about whether my heart's desire was a possibility. Could a gay man find a lifelong partner to love and cherish? I had seen long-term gay couples, but they were few and far between. Most gay men seemed to be focused on short-term relationships— picking up a date at a bar, that sort of thing. Was there ever going to be a man out there for me? A man that I could trust? A man who wouldn't abandon me for a new hookup? A man who wanted all the things that I did—a home, commitment, and a shared future?

For months after the breakup, I withdrew into a very dark place. I enrolled in some classes at OU to finish my undergraduate degree, but I spent most of my time lying on my bed and staring at the ceiling. My thoughts were so painful that I preferred to empty out my brain and vegetate. It's not my nature to lie around and mope, and my parents were plenty concerned. Mother kept urging me to get out, have a social life, see my friends.

So when Jack started coming around, Mother and Daddy were relieved and delighted. They wanted me to find someone who would make me happy, and they could see how happy I was whenever Jack was around.

They did question me about Jack's background because—like all parents—they wanted to be sure that I was dating someone from a "good" family. But I really didn't know what to tell them. Jack was very private about his personal life. I knew that he was born in Chicago, and that after his parents died, he'd gone to a Catholic boarding school. I knew he kept in touch with an older sister named Judy (later changed to Judé). But we were together for almost two years before he ever mentioned anything else about his childhood.

I'm the talkative one. But there wasn't any need for me to tell Jack long stories about my home life because it was the setting of our romance. What was my boyhood in Norman like? Picture a painting by Norman Rockwell. There were five of us McConnell kids, and we were always close-knit. On the holidays, even after some of the older kids were married and in their own homes, we had big family get-togethers.

When Jack and I were dating, my kid sister, Sherre, still lived at home. My big brother Jerry lived nearby. A couple of times a week, Jerry would stop by the house to drop off something or borrow a tool from Daddy. Another of my sisters, Pat, also lived nearby. In addition to family, I had a cozy circle of longtime friends in Norman. At the McConnell house, everybody felt at ease. It's always been like that. When I was a kid, my best friends, the twins Judy and Jayne, used to drop by and say hello. No formality. We all chattered a mile a minute about our lives—what's new, what was happening around town, whatever.

I love to cook, and ever since I was fourteen, Mother was glad to share the role of family chef with me. If I felt like puttering around the kitchen, I might be rolling out pie dough when Jack came over on a Friday night. He would swivel the kitchen stool around, plunk himself down, and lean his gorgeous chin on his strong hands. While I chopped fresh pecans, he'd start talking about his day at work. I'd tell him about my classes as delicious aromas began to waft out of the kitchen. By the time I reached into the oven to pluck out a steaming pie, folks would be gathering around the dining room table. I would barely get the slices onto plates before the notes of conversation turned into the satisfied sounds of hungry folks enjoying wonderful food.

Winter weather in Oklahoma is unpredictable. Nearly every day, the wind blows hard. Sometimes it's cold enough to chill you to the bone. Other days, the sun comes out and drives the temperature up thirty degrees. On those days, the mild breeze feels delightful. On sunny Saturdays, Jack and I took walks around my parents' property. There were large cedar trees at the edges of our yard, and the thick evergreen branches looked magnificent above the red soil. We also had a few pitiful scrub oaks that lost all their leaves in the fall. Their gnarly branches formed twisted sculptures against the sky. Back then, most couples—whether straight or gay—didn't do much touching in front of their parents. But my daddy had built some small sheds on our property for incubating his quail, and Jack and I sometimes ducked inside to get out of the wind. The quail didn't seem to mind if we did a little necking in front of them.

Jack and I are both naturally slim—we don't have the beefy builds of the guys that you see on a football field. Jack always says that he admires lean male bodies. He also likes square jaws and cleft chins—like mine. We wore the same size in clothes and shoes. We both have blue eyes. Ever the romantic, I mused about how the two of us looked like a matched pair—salt and pepper shakers. We were made to be beside each other. I knew I was in love with him. And, like any young lover, I wanted to show off my handsome beau to the world. In my fantasies, we would stroll hand in hand through the streets of my hometown and I would beam at everybody we met.

But although I'm a romantic, I'm not an idiot. Outside my daydreams and the boundaries of my parents' property, Jack and I had to be careful. I knew that. After all, I had lived in Norman all my life, and I had seen what happened to guys who acted "different." There were plenty of bullies at my school, and I could spot their grownup counterparts around town and at church. When I was a tween, I recognized that the hateful sermons delivered from the church pulpit were about people like me. One Sunday as I looked around the congregation, my belly twisted with this realization: these God-fearing souls would gleefully murder me if they knew that I was gay, and they'd do it without pausing to inhale! That was the day I walked out of our family's Baptist church and refused to go back. From then on, I understood how lucky I was that I had never been a victim of some bully's hate. My wonderful family was the source of my security. Starting on the day I entered grade school, my older brother Jerry made sure that nobody messed with me. In our hometown, Jerry was a high school baseball and basketball star, admired by everybody, and he was fiercely protective of me, his kid brother.

I was nineteen when I officially came out. The timing was an accident—my parents discovered that I was gay, and I didn't see any point in denying it. Actually, I had pretty much assumed that my parents already knew. It happened while I was dating Bob. As soon as I met Bob at OU, I developed a huge crush on him. He was smart. He loved books, and he was personable. My parents thought so, too—they knew most of my friends, and they really liked Bob. They liked him so much, in fact, that they invited him to board with us. It seemed like a perfect arrangement: my dad was a barber, so we had enough money to put food on the table, but a little extra would come in handy. We lived close enough to campus that Bob wouldn't have a long commute. We had three bedrooms. My parents had the master bedroom, and my younger sister Sherre lived in one bedroom, so Bob moved into my room.

I guess my parents thought that Bob and I were just friends. But one morning, my father happened to open my door while Bob and I were making love. Daddy looked at us, stunned. Then he left, closing the door behind him. Bob and I had already discussed getting our own apartment, so I had planned to tell my parents about our relationship—I just hadn't gotten around to it. I was still young, and it felt awkward to talk about my romantic relationship with Mother and Daddy.

After Daddy closed the door, I got up and dressed and went into the kitchen. Mother told me that Daddy had already gone to work, but they were going to want to have a talk with me that evening.

That day, Bob and I moved our stuff to a friend's place. Then I went home to talk with my parents. It wasn't a big scene. Mother and Daddy said they had spoken to Jerry, and he suggested that I go see a psychiatrist. In the sixties, that was the usual advice when parents learned their children were gay. I agreed to go—just to make them feel better. But I didn't really see the point. I knew who I was; I had known for as long as I could remember. When I was just a kid, and my best friends, Judy and Jayne, talked about their dreams of love and marriage, my dreams matched theirs. The girls pictured themselves in a sparkling new house with a handsome husband—so did I. Later, when we were in junior high, the girls talked about making out with the cute boys at school. I fantasized about making out with those same cute boys.

The psychiatrist was a knowledgeable scientist and an honest man. After giving me some personality tests, he met with my parents and me in his office. He didn't suggest any crackpot "cures." And he didn't say anything that I didn't already know; his tests showed that I was a stable and well-adjusted young man. He told my parents that they could accept who I was or chase me out of their lives—it was up to them. Mother and Daddy didn't hesitate—they both said they would accept who I was, and the matter was done.

As for the rest of the family—I was still Michael, the same person that I had always been. If I was gay, that was my business. Jerry set the tone. As far as he was concerned, anything I did was my choice, and he wasn't going to interfere.

As accepting as my family was, I understood the climate of the times. When Jack and I dated, I was careful about how we behaved when we were out and about. As our relationship deepened and solidified, I began to wish that we lived someplace where we could be ourselves in front of the whole world. Where we could declare our special bond, just like any other young couple.

We continued dating through the winter months. On March 10, to celebrate his twenty-fifth birthday, Jack invited me to go to *Two for the Seesaw,* a play at the Mummers Theater in Oklahoma City. By then, he was living in Bethany, a western suburb of the city, sharing a house with a pair of gay lovers.

After the play, we went back to Jack's room. The play was light and frothy, and we were in a fizzy mood. Suddenly, Jack got serious and told me that we needed to talk.

"I think we should become lovers," he said.

I grinned from ear to ear. My dream man had just proposed to me! Among gay men, being "lovers" meant moving in together. It was comparable to a straight couple becoming engaged. And it was exactly what I wanted—a committed, long-term, loving relationship.

"Okay," I said, my heart singing. "But I want to get married."

Jack raised his eyebrows. "Married? You and me?"

"Yes," I said. "Married. Legally." I grinned and added,

"Mother and Daddy always told me that I'm as good as anybody else. And the man that I marry better agree. If other couples have the right to marry, so do we."

"Oh." Jack hesitated long enough to take a breath. Then he flashed his movie star smile. "Well, I guess I'm going to have to figure out how we can do that, then."

And that's when we began, in earnest, to plan the world's first gay marriage.

Proud graduates, 1968.

3

Military Maneuvers

• • •

After we committed to each other, Jack left his car with me. That saved him from having to pick me up on the weekends. He was a field engineer so he had the use of a company car to drive himself back and forth to work. My parents were impressed. Clearly, Jack was a young man with a substantial job. By leaving his car for me to drive, it was also clear that he was serious about me.

In June, Jack and I moved into a one-bedroom apartment in a little cluster of duplexes on Drake Circle, on the southeastern edge of Norman. It was an easy walk to campus—just a few blocks—so most of the apartments were rented by college students. I was very familiar with the area. When I was a kid, it had been a big dairy farm where my family got our milk, and I used to ride my horse out there.

Our apartment was about two years old, and everything looked practically new. It had a large walk-in closet off the bedroom, a living room, a kitchen/dining area, a patio, and a carport out front. It came furnished with the basics—a couch, a few chairs, lamps, and tables in the living room; a dining room table and four chairs in the eating area. We even had a grill on our patio. Best of all, the place had air conditioning.

It was perfect for us. I had already decided to apply for graduate school at OU, and I could walk to my classes. I got interested in library science back when I lived with Bob, and I wanted to get my master's degree and be a librarian. Jack had been offered a better-paying position as an engineer at Tinker Air Force Base, and the base was a quick drive on a county road from our new apartment. In July, he started his new job.

We had lots of friends in both Norman and Oklahoma City. On weekends, we enjoyed going to movies and plays and clubs, or I would give our little kitchen a workout by preparing an elaborate meal for a couple of our friends. It was a happy, busy time in our lives.

In August—about a month after Jack took the job at Tinker Air Force Base—he got a manila envelope in the mail. It contained his official discharge from the armed forces. I knew Jack had been in the Air Force before we met, from 1959 through 1963. I also knew that he'd left active duty early—before finishing his six-year officer commitment—because a complaint had been registered against him. But I didn't know anything about military procedures. I was surprised that after all these years, Jack was still getting official military paperwork in the mail.

Jack opened the envelope and pulled out the document. I saw his jaw clamp.

"What's wrong?" I asked.

"It's a general discharge," he said. "The Air Force just replaced my honorable discharge with a general discharge."

"So?"

He shrugged. "Could be trouble."

Jack had already told me the story of his early discharge. There'd been a misunderstanding—Jack had misread the signals given by another airman. Jack thought the fellow was flirting, so Jack invited him to go to bed. The airman, who insisted he was straight, was offended. Instead of laughing off the incident, the fellow complained. As a result, the Air Force stopped processing its promise to award Jack an officer's commission. Jack then requested release from his promise to serve an additional two years, and it was granted. Before Jack left the base, his commander handed him a certificate of honorable discharge.

At the time, Jack thought it was no big deal. In fact, he thought it was a blessing in disguise. The military had paid for Jack to take engineering classes at OU while he was enlisted. By the time the complaint was lodged, Jack had finished his coursework and earned his degree. The early release from active duty meant that Jack didn't need to delay his engineering career while completing his officer commission.

Jack explained to me that a general discharge is not the same as an honorable discharge. It's military code for "something is wrong." It's a way to wave a red flag at future employers. In other words, it's a form of harassment. The Air Force was playing the part of a bully.

Sure enough, a copy of this general discharge was sent to Jack's boss at Tinker Air Force Base, who informed Jack that he was ineligible to work at a military facility. His choice: resign or be fired. He resigned.

"This is a game that two can play," Jack said, on the

day that he carried home the box containing his belongings from work. His eyes were flashing like hammered flint.

I knew he was angry about what the Air Force had done to him. But with his usual resilience, Jack moved right along with his life. He'd been thinking about getting a graduate degree anyway, and now he had the time to go back to school. He enrolled in Oklahoma City University's MBA program at night. To support himself, he worked days at the Lone Star Brewery in Oklahoma City. The work was easy enough. Jack moved beer crates into coolers, cleaned floors, and did whatever was needed. And the money was great since it was paid on a union scale.

Jack had no intention of leaving a permanent stain on his record, so he began investigating how he could get the honorable discharge reinstated. The first thing he did was meet with our U.S. representative, John Jarman. Although Jarman promised he would look into the matter, his office dropped it. Jack also contacted an attorney at the American Legion. But the attorney didn't seem willing to act either.

During the fall and winter of 1967–68, we were so busy that we simply didn't have any time to play games with the military. I was doing my graduate coursework in library science at OU while Jack was going to school at night and working at the brewery. So Jack decided to put his duel with the Air Force on pause for the time being.

We could also see that the American landscape was changing around us. The signs were everywhere: young people were taking to the streets to demand that the United States end its involvement in the Vietnam War, that black people receive equal treatment under the law, that women be treated as equals in the workplace and in the home. We wanted to play our parts in this cultural earthquake. As soon as we had time to consider the best strategy, Jack would make his move against the Air Force.

While I lived with Jack, I began to learn about the idiosyncrasies of my intended husband. For instance, although we're both good students, our study styles are completely different. Jack thrives on structure and discipline. Using planks of wood and metal poles, he built himself a spartan desk and shelves in our bedroom's walk-in closet. He lined up his textbooks and his clock on the shelves, and he assigned himself two hours of study at that desk every evening. Even on weekends, he refused to go out until he had put in his two hours of study time. I take a more fluid approach to my work. Library science suited my academic interests to a T, and the new information seemed to slide effortlessly into my head. When I needed to crack the books, I did. When I didn't, I experimented with new recipes.

In the spring of 1968, we were both graduating from our master's degree programs—one week apart. Jack's graduation came first, and I planned a candlelight dinner for the two of us to celebrate. I flipped through cookbooks until I found what looked to be a mouth-watering recipe for marinating steaks, and I made a list of the ingredients that I would need.

As I was carrying in the groceries on the afternoon before his graduation ceremony, I heard Jack talking on our phone.

"It's Judy," he mouthed to me. He hung up and announced, "She's here for my graduation. Some of my other sisters are here, too."

I looked at him, dumbfounded. I knew Jack had a sister named Judy, but this was the first I'd heard of other sisters. I opened my mouth to tell him that I would need to pick up more steaks if we were having company, but I never got the chance. Jack stuffed the car keys in his pocket and hurried out of the room.

"She says they're excited because I'm the first one in our family to graduate from college. They decided to surprise me," he called from the living room.

I heard the door open.

"I've got to go deal with this," he said.

I heard the door slam.

That was the end of our special candlelight dinner. Jack never even called to let me know his plans for the rest of the weekend. When I realized that my husband-to-be had gone off to his graduation ceremony without me, I heaved the damn steaks in the trash and called a friend to come pick me up. I was fuming.

That week, Jack didn't utter a single word about his graduation weekend, and I certainly wasn't going to give him the satisfaction of asking. I made arrangements to celebrate my graduation in the company of my own family the following week, and I did not invite Jack to join us. I thought that would show him that I was furious. That he had really hurt my feelings. That if he ever acted so horribly again, he would be sleeping on the couch until his toes froze. Instead, many years later, I discovered that Jack never gave the incident a second thought. Ever the logical, emotionless engineer, he simply assumed that I preferred to celebrate my graduation with my own family and without him. (Believe me, there are moments when I wonder why I ever wanted to marry an engineer!)

After that, I started to ask questions about Jack's background. I mean, what kind of man never mentions that he has six sisters and three brothers? Nine siblings! Jack was the youngest of ten kids. By the time he came along, six of the older Baker kids had already left home and started their own families. One of the older sisters was a nun. She had actually taken Jack's given name, Richard, as her convent name and was called Sister Ann Richard for the rest of her life. Richard is Jack's full name—Richard John Baker— but he's always preferred to go by nicknames. By the time I met him, he liked to be called Jack, but when he was a kid, his family called him Rich, and when he started work as an engineer, his colleagues called him Dick.

I probed further. The more I learned about Jack's childhood, the more it sounded like the opening chapter of a novel by Dickens—with a title like *The Bleak Boy*. His mother died when he was four, and he had no memory of her at all. His dad died when he was five. At the age of six, Jack was an orphan in a Catholic boarding school near Chicago, later named Maryville Academy. He remained there until his graduation from high school at age seventeen. His sister Katy, one year older than he was, also went to Maryville. So did his sister Judy, who was two grades ahead of him in school but his favorite family playmate. One brother, Joe, also went to Maryville, but Joe was already a teenager when their parents died, and he showed no interest in his kid brother. Although the older siblings occasionally visited Maryville, Jack really had only one constant and loving adult to support him—his mother's mother. This grandmother came to visit him twice each month, which was as often as the boarding school allowed.

No wonder Jack often seemed cold and unemotional—the poor fellow had been practically abandoned by his relatives to a life among strangers at a Catholic boarding school. Coming from the warm nest of my own loving family, I was horrified.

"How did you feel about living at Maryville?" I asked him, my voice hushed to a whisper. I'm sure my eyes were brimming with tears.

"I enjoyed it there," he said.

I must have looked stupified. "You enjoyed living at a Catholic boarding school?"

"Of course," Jack grinned. "It was an all-male dormitory. The nuns fed me, and the priests thought I was a smart little fellow. I always had plenty of kids to play with."

"But didn't you miss your family?"

Jack shrugged. "Well, Judy was at Maryville, so I got to see her. I hardly knew most of the others."

"But you didn't have a home." I couldn't bear the thought of my lover growing up in such a cold, impersonal environment.

"Well, I always wished that I had access to a refrigerator, like kids do at home," Jack said. "Not that they didn't feed me at Maryville. But you know how young boys are—always hungry. Then again, it was a blessing in disguise. That's probably how I learned to keep myself slim."

"That's the only thing you wished you had?" I said. "A refrigerator?"

He paused, as if he was remembering something else. "Well, I didn't like the sleeping schedule. The nuns made us stay in bed until five, but I was always awake by two or three in the morning. I hated having to lie there. There wasn't anything to do but listen to the birds. But I figured out how to get around that rule."

I perked up, thinking I was about to hear a tale of schoolboy mischief. "How?"

"I volunteered to be the altar boy at early mass," Jack said. "Nobody else wanted to do that because you had to get up by four to prepare for the 5 a.m. mass. But I loved that. And then I got to eat breakfast with the employees, and their food was always better. So it was a great arrangement." Jack laughed. "The priests loved me, and they made sure that nobody hassled me. I guess they thought I would become a priest when I grew up because I liked being an altar boy so much."

I shook my head at the wonder of it. What would those priests think of their little altar boy now that he'd grown up and gotten engaged to his male lover? Well, I thought, that explains it. Jack's childhood must be the reason he always seemed so different from the other gay men that I had known.

As we were completing our graduate degrees, Jack and I began applying for jobs. He was offered an engineering job at a cellophane plant owned by the DuPont Company. It was located in Tecumseh, a small Kansas town halfway between Lawrence and Topeka. That was perfect! I had lived in Lawrence with Bob, and I knew it was a lively college town, the home of the University of Kansas, and reasonably friendly to gays. In fact, I still had some friends there and in Kansas City as well. So I applied for a job as a librarian at Park College, a private college in a suburb of Kansas City, Missouri, and landed the job. I would be working in technical services—acquisitions, periodicals, and later cataloging. The pay was great; of all the graduates in my program, my job offered the second-highest salary. And the work looked like it would be challenging and interesting. Jack and I decided we would find a place to live in Lawrence, partway between our work places.

As we got ready to move, we continued talking about the other items on what we had begun to call our agenda: high on that list was my desire to get married. For real. Openly and with a legal license. If we were going to do that, we needed to learn about the law. And it was time for Jack to make the next move in his duel with the Air Force. For that, we realized that we also needed to know more about the law.

Jack was eligible to go to school on the G.I. Bill, and he was intrigued by the idea of law school. He already held degrees in engineering and in business. With a license to practice law, he would have a formidable resumé. He had always pictured himself working for a big corporation or maybe even starting his own business. We began seriously talking about him going back to school for his law degree.

Jack in Lawrence, Kansas, 1969. Photograph by Terry C. Vanderplas.

4

Forcing the Air Force to Fly Fair

. . . .

In June 1968, we piled our clothes and books into our VW Beetle and drove to our new home in Lawrence, Kansas. We had found a furnished two-bedroom apartment to rent. It was spacious, the upstairs floor in a duplex, and in one of the city's nicest neighborhoods. Other DuPont engineers lived nearby. Since we would be commuting in different directions during the week, we needed separate cars, so I got a VW for myself. And just to be sure that we always had a vehicle in working order, we bought a used Plymouth to serve as a backup.

It was a glorious time, and both of us paddled happily into our new lives. In addition to his job, Jack enrolled in a statistics course in the University of Kansas night school—just to keep his mind active. On the nights that Jack went to his statistics course, I worked at the reference desk at the Park College library. I loved my work as a librarian. For me, doing research is exciting; it's a mental treat as well as a natural strength.

We enjoyed a steady stream of visiting friends from across the country, especially friends from OU. I also started looking up people I had known when I lived in Lawrence with Bob. I was pleased to find so many of them still in town. Soon we were enjoying weekend barbeque cookouts and get-togethers for drinks or dinner. Our life fell into a busy, comfortable pattern. During the week, we went to work and then returned home to share dinner and time together. On the weekends, we socialized, attended special events at the university or around town, and took care of chores at our apartment.

On weekends, Jack and I occasionally went on excursions to Kansas City. It was fun to explore the city's gay bars. Back then, bars were the center of gay social life. Other than private homes and parties, bars were the only places where gay men and women could be themselves—laugh and dance, meet and chat in relative safety.

A lot of people go to bars to meet someone new and hook up. I'm not going to pretend that Jack and I never indulged in this. As young men, and even after we committed to spend our lives together, we sometimes enjoyed sexual encounters with handsome fellows we met at bars or elsewhere. During the height of the sexual revolution in the seventies, when gay bathhouses were springing up in cities large and small, we occasionally visited these as well. In the bathhouses, sexual encounters were usually the evening's entertainment. (Not that it was mandatory to have sex—some people just enjoyed feasting their eyes on all those good-looking male bodies.) When Jack and I were apart, when one of us was away on a business trip or something, it was understood that we were free to date other men.

Back then, whenever the topic of marriage was brought

up, there were heated discussions in the gay community about sexual fidelity. A lot of young people—straight as well as gay—were glorying in "free love." They didn't want to feel shackled by traditional marriages. Some people even argued that marriage was an outmoded institution that repressed the human spirit and denied biological reality. I think it's best to get this subject on the table and be open about it.

Jack and I believe there are important emotional benefits from forming a stable, lifelong relationship. And of course we both feel that gay men and women are entitled to the same legal and financial benefits as any other married couple. For us, sexual exclusivity was not one of the "rules" of being married. We love each other; we don't own each other. From the day when we pledged to spend our lives together, I trusted Jack. There simply wasn't any reason to get jealous or hurt if he did have a sexual encounter with another man. I knew that he'd make the best choices for himself without jeopardizing what we were building together. I am not downplaying the importance of physical intimacy. I believe that sharing intimacy has big implications. I'm just saying that in any relationship, there needs to be mutual agreement. Our commitment was about love; sexual exclusivity was not a requirement.

Naturally, as we grew older, bathhouses and gay bars and sexual flirtations had less appeal for us. In the years after we left Kansas, we became heavily involved in activism for gay rights, and our days and nights were jammed with meetings and activities. We were too worn out to carry on much of a social life. And later, our focus turned inward—to ourselves, the home that we were creating, our close friends, our jobs and goals. Over the years, the general cultural climate changed, too. After AIDS was identified, any discussion about sexual matters had to consider safety as well as beliefs and desires. But when we committed to spend our life together, Jack and I talked about what we expected from our relationship, and we both felt comfortable with our arrangement.

In Lawrence, one of our favorite leisure hangouts was the Rock Chalk Cafe, a counterculture beer joint near campus. We enjoyed the casual atmosphere of this popular gathering spot as well as its rich stew of patrons, which included students and professors, hippies and local residents. It was a small, crowded, dimly lit place with a bar, some wooden tables and booths, and neon beer signs decorating the walls. We thought it was a great place to relax and have a beer, catch up with old friends or meet some interesting newcomer. While we were there, I would often pick up one of the alternative newspapers that were piled in stacks by the door so I could check out what was playing around town or in Kansas City.

That's probably how I happened on an announcement about an upcoming conference, the North American Conference of Homophile Organizations. Although I'd never heard of this particular organization, I knew there was a gay activist group in Kansas City, and I figured this conference might be a way for us to link up with gay men and women who were interested in social change, like us.

"Hey, Jack, look." I showed him the notice. The conference would take place in August at a Kansas City hotel. "Maybe we should drive over?"

Jack scanned the item. "There's a session on government discrimination against gays," he said, nodding. "Maybe we'll meet someone who knows how to deal with the Air Force."

We were already familiar with the part of town where the conference was held. It was down the street from a popular gay bar, the Arabian Nights. Jack and I usually called that place "The Tent" because of its over-the-top décor. We drove over on the morning of the conference and registered when we got there.

Only about fifteen or twenty people were in the meeting room, most of them middle-aged men. Jack and I were probably the youngest people attending. The main speaker was Frank Kameny, one of the founders of the Mattachine Society in Washington, D.C. Jack and I knew a little about the Mattachine Society. It formed in Los Angeles in 1950 as a secret social organization for left-wing gay men, then gained notice and membership when it defended a member who had been arrested for lewd behavior. Over the next decade, branches sprang up in several big cities, and they battled sodomy laws, discrimination against gays in the work force, and police harassment. The Mattachine Society was one of those early groups that are often considered precursors to the modern gay rights movement.

Kameny explained his personal involvement in what he called the homophile movement: he had been an astronomer for the U.S. Army until his homosexuality was discovered in 1957 and he lost his job. He had mounted an antidiscrimination suit against the government and taken it all the way to the U.S. Supreme Court. When we met him at the conference, Kameny was forty-three years old, a trim man, both intelligent and intense. He reminded me of some of my undergraduate chemistry and microbiology professors. After losing his job, Kameny devoted himself to defending gays—whom he preferred to call "homophiles"—against discrimination. During a break in the session, Jack and I stopped him in the hall outside the meeting room. We told him about Jack's problem with the Air Force. Kameny listened carefully. I was impressed by how quickly he grasped the essence of our situation. He agreed that Jack should not submit to living under the shadow of a general discharge. There was no justification for the Air Force's action— Jack had not breached national security or been derelict in his duties. This was harassment, pure and simple, and it could harm Jack's future job prospects. Kameny advised Jack to write a letter requesting legal representation from the American Civil Liberties Union in Washington, D.C., and to mention Kameny's name.

Jack sent his letter on September 26, 1968, to Ralph Temple, the director of the Washington, D.C., arm of the ACLU. When he didn't hear anything, he sent a follow-up letter on December 23. Jack kept Kameny informed about the case.

On January 14, 1969, Kameny called Jack with good news: the ACLU would take the case. In February, Jack received a letter from Mr. Temple requesting him to send copies of all his "essential correspondence" to Stuart Land, who was the volunteer attorney from the Arnold and Porter law firm who would be representing him. Kameny wrote to congratulate Jack and tell him that his attorney was at a top firm—Arnold and Porter was formerly known as Arnold, Porter, and Fortas, because it had included Abe

Fortas until he was appointed a justice of the U.S. Supreme Court.

At last, the game was on.

Meanwhile, we kept thinking about the other items on our agenda. We began poring over law school catalogs for Jack. During the winter, we visited the University of Minnesota campus in Minneapolis and toured the University of Chicago campus.

Jack's sister Judy lived on the south side of Chicago, so we stopped by to see her. Her husband Gene was a repairman for the Sears, Roebuck and Company, and they lived in a modest row house with their four little kids. Judy met us at the door and gave Jack a big hug. I could tell how proud she was of her smart, handsome kid brother. As soon as she got both of us seated and comfortable, she started telling Jack all the news about their many siblings. Judy was almost as tall as Jack, and she had a down-to-earth style. She wore no makeup, and her brown hair was short and simple rather than the popular bouffant hairstyle of the time. She wasn't a flashy dresser either. While she chattered about the family, I compared her features with Jack's. Although there's an obvious bond of affection between them, they don't look alike. Jack has only one photo of his parents, and I'm always struck by how much he resembles his handsome father. Judy, on the other hand, reminds me of his pretty, sweet-faced mother.

A few months later, Jack was accepted by two fine law schools: the University of Minnesota and the University of Kansas. We thought the U of M was the better choice. One of our friends had lived in Minneapolis and described how liberal and progressive that city was, with a lively gay community. Plus, I love cold weather, so I thought the Minnesota climate would be preferable to living in Kansas with its brutal summers.

To celebrate Jack's acceptance, I went shopping and spent way too much on a thick, gorgeous sweater to keep my lover warm during the long Minneapolis winter. It was a beige crewneck pullover in luxurious mohair, knit all over with thick cables. Jack thanked me for it, but I'm sure that he didn't appreciate the gift because I discovered, when I moved to Minneapolis a year later, that he'd never so much as taken it out of the drawer. (No wonder he developed a terrible cold that practically turned into pneumonia during his very first winter there. If I hadn't been so worried about him, I would've told him that it served him right!)

The one downside of our choice of law schools was that we would have to live in separate cities for a year. When I started my job at Park College, I had signed a two-year contract, and I wouldn't be able to relocate until the summer of 1970.

Meanwhile, in June, Jack got a letter informing him that the Air Force Discharge Review Board would hear his case on July 15. The ACLU attorney wanted Jack to meet with him in Washington, D.C., on the day before the hearing. Kameny invited Jack to stay at his home.

When Jack returned from that trip, he told me all about the experience. It was eye-opening for both of us. Stuart Land had written down every word that he planned to say at the hearing. At his meeting with Jack, Land went over his script and checked each fact. Jack thought that with such careful preparation, the case would be resolved quickly in Jack's favor. But nothing conclusive actually happened at the hearing. Land argued that Jack had been denied due process. To prove this, he needed access to the reports filed by the original Air Force review board. These were sealed, so Land requested them.

It took almost two months for the Air Force to act on the request. Finally, on September 4, Land called Jack to say that the Air Force had rejected their request for records. Land, of course, advised an appeal.

Jack hadn't yet begun his law school classes, but this hearing provided him with a sneak peek at the circuitous workings of the legal system. We began to understand that games played in a court of law move at about the same pace as a glacier. It was a lesson that would be reinforced many times in the years to come as we battled other instances of discrimination against gay men. I've come to think of it like this: Every game requires practice. When you play a game on a tennis court, you practice your forehand, and when you play a game on a basketball court, you practice your free throw. Playing the game in a court of law requires you to practice patience. No problem for me, I thought. Librarians are patient people.

These MONTHS
without you ARE
becoming too
unbearable

Mike McConnell
3900 Charlotte
Kansas City Missouri

Postcard from Jack, November 18, 1969. Courtesy of the Jean-Nickolaus Tretter Collection in GLBT Studies, University of Minnesota Libraries.

5

Jack Moves Away

· · · · ·

As we neared the end of September 1969, when Jack's law school classes would begin, I found myself sweeping aside waves of emotion. Later, I told myself, think about it later—there's so much that needs to be done first. No time to dwell on doubts, Michael. Just get the boxes packed, get the arrangements made. But worries kept lapping at the edge of my mind. Were we making the right decision? We truly loved the home we had made for ourselves in Lawrence. We had friends, satisfying work, a great apartment. Was it really a good idea to unsettle everything? To live apart for an entire year?

At other moments, I found myself tingling with excitement. This is real; it's going to happen! Every breath I have ever taken has led me to this moment. We are going to marry each other, legally and openly. To reach our cherished goal, I knew that we had to set sail on uncharted seas, and we needed vital knowledge to navigate our journey. That's why Jack was going to law school. That's why we had to be apart for a year. It's only a year, I told myself—it will be over before I know it.

I wouldn't need our spacious apartment anymore, so we found a smaller place for me to live in Kansas City near Park College. We located an apartment in Minneapolis near campus for Jack. We sorted our stuff into piles—what Jack would need to bring with him and what I would take to my new place.

As we worked, the doubts came cascading back; I loved Jack and I believed in his love for me, but a year seemed an eternity. Jack would be taking classes, meeting brilliant people, and living in a dynamic city. I would be working at the same job at Park College, hanging out in the same places with the same friends. How would our relationship stand the strain? How would I bear the emptiness without him?

In the third week of September, Jack and I finished packing the last of our boxes. We carried his clothes out to his VW. We loaded the rest of his stuff into my car to store at my new place. I would be living in an efficiency unit in an old mansion on Rockhill Road in Kansas City. It was located in a beautiful, park-like area of the city, with a convenient freeway commute to Park College. Situated near art museums, upscale shops, some of our closest friends, and two gay bars, the tiny apartment was perfectly suited to my every need—except that Jack wouldn't be living there with me.

After moving my stuff into my new place, Jack and I spent the night there. The next day, we took off in two cars to get him settled in Minneapolis.

That was a long, hard drive. I kept telling myself to buck up. Save your tears for the drive back. Once in Minneapolis, we quickly unloaded Jack's car and got him situated. His apartment was relatively barren, but Jack was fine with it. He had the basics, and he figured he would be too busy with his studies to worry about much else. We spent one night there together, and the next morning I was on the road back to Kansas City. I had to be at work the next day so there wasn't time to linger.

Before we parted, we made all the usual assurances to each other—that we would write as often as possible, that we would visit each other often and soon, that we would always love each other. But it nearly killed me to say good-bye.

Back then, long-distance phone calls were costly, so our calls were carefully planned and far too infrequent. The world hadn't yet converted to e-mail; we mostly carried on our love affair with the help of the post office.

Jack made his own picture postcards by gluing a black-and-white cartoon clipped from the newspaper onto a white index card. The cartoon was called "love is," and it featured a cute little naked boy and girl. On each strip, the caption completes a sentence that begins with the title, like "love is . . . thinking about him all the time he's away." Jack sometimes crossed out the cartoon's words and substituted his own in red ink so the captions would mirror our situation. All around the cartoon, he'd print everyday news in the tiniest of handwriting. He alternated between black and red ink so the separate items would be distinguishable. Mostly, he wrote about his classes and activities. He let the cartoon captions convey the mushy stuff about how much he loved and missed me.

I sent Jack handwritten letters. I often tore off sheets of lined paper from a half-sized yellow pad measuring five by eight inches. I don't know why we both decided to write on small-sized paper. Maybe it felt more like we were

whispering—as though we were sharing the intimate se-
crets of lovers rather than sending public messages. I usually dashed off my letters quickly, filling both sides with
my scribbled words—as if by giving my fingers a workout,
I could warm up the chill that Jack's absence left inside me.
My letters alternated between reports of everyday news
and paragraphs in which I explored my feelings for him.

We decided that we would visit once a month, and
I did most of the traveling because I knew that Jack was
swamped with reading and studying for his classes. I arranged my work schedule so I had one long weekend a
month available for a trip to Minneapolis. On holidays,
Jack sometimes managed to carve out enough time to make
it down to Kansas City. Each time we spent a weekend together, my letters became more passionate. In December,
I wrote: "Jack, I don't want to sound all mushy and dumb
but . . . I am simply overwhelmed by the change (or if
there's been no change—the outward expression) of your
attitude to our relationship and especially to me. You are
giving me everything I need to function as a whole human
being for the first time in my life. It doesn't make me any
happier to be so far away from you, but it does help the
loneliness I feel so often now."

When I was in Kansas City, I tried to keep my mind
stuffed full of details and duties so there was no room to
dwell on how much I missed Jack. Although there were
people all around me, nobody was a substitute for Jack. He
was the one I longed to talk with and hold. I dated a sweet
fellow in Lawrence during the fall, but I let him know
from the start that our relationship would not become permanent because I had a serious boyfriend in another city.

I knew that Jack was also dating a guy in Minneapolis. Neither of us talked about these dates. They were just a way to curb the hollow feelings until we could resume our life together.

After I had been living alone in the Rockhill Road efficiency for a few months, a friend named Clint Critchfield asked if I would consider moving in with him in a house near the University of Missouri, Kansas City; it wasn't too far from my efficiency. Clint traveled quite a bit in his job, so I would still have plenty of time to myself. Frankly, I wasn't faring all that well living alone. I was beginning to flounder without Jack. I missed him terribly.

Sharing a house with Clint made a huge difference in my outlook. He was gone a lot, but he was good company when he was home. We had some friends in common, and since we occupied a whole house, our place became something of a gathering spot for our overlapping circles. Just having somebody living in the house with me gave me a sense of security. I didn't feel as much like I was drifting. We fitted the house up with furniture and accessories from both our collections, and it looked nice and homey. Clint had a great sound system. And it was handy to have a large storage area in the garage for my other belongings and Jack's stuff.

Clint and I threw a Christmas party on Saturday, December 13. I usually love a party, but I found myself relieved when the last of our guests left around 11:30 p.m. Clint went out to barhop with some of our guests, but I opted to stay home and clean up. When I wrote to tell Jack about the party, I noted that I hadn't dropped by a bar, not even for a quick drink, since before Thanksgiving.

In January, I wrote, "You've shown me what love really is." It seemed to me that my love for Jack was growing deeper roots during this long, icy winter of deprivation. Our relationship had entered a period of hibernation, and when we emerged, our bond would be much stronger. I imagined myself starving like a hibernating bear—not for food but for Jack.

I think Jack felt the same growth in our love. In January, he sent me a long letter that was uncharacteristically emotional. "I was sitting here daydreaming," he wrote. "I thought you might enjoy a letter instead of a postcard."

There is at least one good aspect of our being apart. It has made me realize more than ever before how much I really do love you. I guess it's true that we tend to take things for granted—until we lose them. Last summer I was beginning to doubt the stability of our relationship & was in a way looking forward to the forthcoming separation so that I could be alone & contemplate.

I began to realize gradually how much I really depended on you emotionally for support & how much my life was empty without you. I was "FREE again" but as the song goes, there was something missing. I missed you more each day. . . . The more I thought about you & our relationship the more I realized how "society" had kept me from really enjoying life by forcing a double life on me. It was because of you that I decided to unmask *completely* & demand respect. I haven't regretted that decision but instead have found a different type of happiness in finding real friends. It gives me tremendous pleasure to talk about my lover. . . . It's as tho I've seen the sky for the first time.

Oddly, the longer we were apart, the less interested I was in physical intimacy with others. In February, I wrote to Jack: "It's really strange how my sex attitudes have changed since you moved to Minnesota. I don't feel the frustration about sex that I used to. Now I'm trying to decide if it's a result of my age or my mental attitude. It's amazing how much I think about having sex with you. You are delicious!"

I'm pretty sure that Jack didn't withdraw from social life as much as I did. In the same month that I wrote about my nearly celibate existence, Jack mentioned that he'd contracted crabs (pubic lice)! He wondered if he'd picked them up from me. (He didn't.)

In March, I wrote him: "You always give me the sense of direction and well-being that I need." By April, all I could do was think about being by his side, and I wrote: "There isn't much time left before I'll be sleeping with you and seeing you every day. I'm so excited at the prospects for the future that I feel I'm going through a rebirth. I really feel as if my life is going to just begin. I'm just panting for June."

By spring, I had a job lined up in Minneapolis. We had a plan for getting our marriage license, and we began to talk about our wedding ceremony. We even enlisted friends to help with some of the details—the ring, the invitations. At last, the long cold winter of deprivation was over. We were about to embark on our future.

Jack dancing with me at the first FREE dance at the U of M, 1970.
Photograph by Paul Hagen.

6

FREE

. . . . . .

During our separation, Jack and I both maintained busy schedules. In Kansas, I plunged into my work, partly to keep my sanity and partly because I love library work. While Jack did law research as a student in Minneapolis, I created my own research projects at the library. I compiled bibliographies on current topics such as black history, focusing on the civil rights movement. Of course, I was especially interested in anything involving gay rights. I kept track of cases involving discrimination against gays, and I researched gay liberation efforts budding around the country and the world. News about kindred souls inspired me.

As a student, Jack plunged headlong into the emerging gay pride movement on campus at the University of Minnesota. Although he never had time to participate in campus life when he was taking classes for his engineering and business degrees, he always wished that he had. He was being supported by the G.I. Bill during law school, and I urged him to get into campus life. Jack had always worked so hard; I felt he deserved some of the perks that came with being young. In his letters to me, Jack often mentioned his involvement with campus events.

Before he left for law school, Jack and I had read about the first gay student organization in the country, which was established in 1967 at Columbia University. Jack mused about forming a similar group on the U of M campus. But when he arrived in Minneapolis, he saw an article in the city's daily morning newspaper, the *Tribune,* about Welcome Week events on campus and learned that such a group had already formed. It was called FREE, an acronym for Fight Repression of Erotic Expression, and its stated mission was "to free people from outdated, damaging moral restrictions." FREE was formed as an offshoot of an off-campus course, "The Homosexual Revolution," which had been taught in May 1969 by Koreen Phelps and Stephen Ihrig. The course met in a coffeehouse on the West Bank as part of the alternative education offered by a group called the Minnesota Free University.

In October, Jack and about forty others attended a meeting at Coffman Memorial Union to make FREE an officially sanctioned student organization, which would give it the right to use campus facilities. To be a student organization, FREE needed a constitution and student officers. Jack suggested that they request advice from the university's Legal Aid Clinic, and he helped draft the constitution. At the next meeting, he became the first president of the new campus club.

Until this point, FREE had sponsored informal social gatherings, such as picnics and potluck dinners. These gatherings were valuable because they gave newcomers like Jack a way to make friends with other gays in the area and they removed the university's gay social scene from the fast-sex atmosphere of the downtown gay bars. By providing gays with an alternative way to socialize, FREE went a long way toward creating a feeling of self-dignity as well as a sense of community.

As soon as the University's Senate Committee on Student Affairs approved FREE as a student organization, the group requested the use of campus facilities for a gay dance. It would be the country's first gay dance on a campus. To Jack's surprise, the university granted routine permission. The dance was a small, quiet affair, held on October 28 in the student union's Whole Coffeehouse. It went smoothly and received no notoriety. But when FREE placed an ad in the student newspaper to get out the word about a second dance on November 19, the university's news service noticed and promptly alerted area media. Four local newspapers covered the November dance. In their stories, the reporters introduced the leaders of FREE, including Jack. The wire services picked up the story, and it was run in newspapers far from the Twin Cities, including the *Washington Post*.

Jack started urging the members of FREE to do more than just arrange parties. As president, he envisioned the organization as a dynamic agent of social change. He wrote me a note to this effect and added his personal goal: "We're going to move swiftly." Perhaps because Jack was older and had already decided who he was and declared it to the world, he was ready for bold action. He had begun his own battle with the Air Force about his discharge. Now he wanted FREE to lead and confront, to change laws as well as attitudes.

Unlike most of the members of FREE, Jack wasn't afraid of the spotlight. He was willing to be named, quoted, and photographed by reporters. And that's exactly what happened. Due to frequent references to him in the newspaper, Jack began to be contacted by the media as if he were the official spokesman for the gays on campus. From afar, I watched with amusement as my lover became something of a local media star. Jack was handsome, with that great smile that had first attracted me back at the barn dance in Norman. He was clean-cut. Nothing about his appearance would seem weird or distasteful to the average American. He had a quick mind and a clear speaking voice, and these abilities made him a powerful speaker. He was energetic and capable of juggling several projects simultaneously. And he'd worked in corporate America, so he understood how much reporters appreciate polite and prompt responses.

I was so proud to read about my smart lover opening Minnesota's closets and letting in the fresh air of truth—I only wished that I was beside him, helping him turn all those rusted old doorknobs!

During his first few months in Minneapolis, Jack became more and more impressed by the power of the press. I remember him telling me, one weekend, his eyes dancing with excitement, that "one single news story can bring the gay pride movement into the homes of three and a half million people in Minnesota, including small rural communities where people have never thought about this kind of thing before."

With his background in engineering and business, Jack truly appreciated the effectiveness of media coverage. He decided that the fastest and cheapest way to advance gay rights was to keep the movement newsworthy. In fact, during his months with FREE, Jack began to develop a strategy for the gay pride movement. He called it "steam-pipe politics" because it reminded him of throwing icy water on a hot steam pipe.

"That's how you get people to pay attention," he said to me on one of my first visits with him in Minneapolis. "When the pipe hisses and sizzles, the public is reacting to a hot issue. Then you keep the pressure on. You try to cause a backlash. If enough pressure builds, the pipe will crack." Jack snapped his fingers to demonstrate. "Then all kinds of irrational ideas—ideas buried deep inside the plumbing of people's minds—can pour out and run right down the drain."

I giggled. "Yup, that's where a lot of people's ideas belong—in the sewer." I was thinking about the spiteful people that I had met over the years, starting at my child-hood Baptist church.

With Jack as president, FREE continued hosting dances and potlucks as well as handing out literature around cam-pus. Reporters regularly covered their events. A major TV network (ABC) shot some footage at the gay Thanks-giving dance and ran it on the *Huntley-Brinkley Report* on New Year's Eve. After the campus newspaper, the *Min-nesota Daily,* ran a feature about FREE across its centerfold on January 27, the steam pipe showed signs that it was about to crack: at the February Board of Regents meet-ing, a regent named Fred Hughes introduced a motion to investigate the paper's "tastelessness." Hughes cited, in particular, the centerfold story on FREE. In an article printed in the same paper, he was quoted as saying that such coverage had "put people who live a normal life on the defensive." The regents also directed the student affairs office to investigate how student organizations received university status, implying that they were going to try and overturn FREE's campus status. Meanwhile, Thom Higgins, a radio announcer at St. Paul's station for the blind, was fired for announcing his affiliation with FREE.

FREE now had three flagrant instances of discrimination to battle, and the group became more militant. Members began picketing Higgins's employer. They attended the "straight" dances at the student union and danced openly—boy with boy and girl with girl. St. Stephen's Catholic Church in south Minneapolis offered to host gay dances, and FREE gladly accepted in order to forge a bond with a religious organization. FREE began investigating the hiring practices of the university and local firms to uncover instances of discrimination against gays.

I was thrilled to see Jack's steam-pipe politics in action. Under the constant pressure, attitudes really seemed to be changing. In April 1970, the *Tribune* took a stand in favor of FREE: it ran an editorial decrying discrimination "because of homosexuality."

But pressures within FREE were also threatening to cause an explosion. The original founders, Koreen and Stephen, never dreamed of creating such a fast-paced, highly structured group, a group with both public and political profiles. Koreen and Stephen were comfortable operating in looser gatherings. They had created FREE as a meeting place, a cozy atmosphere where gays could get used to their identities, an ongoing "rap group" (discussion group) that provided moral support.

One incident demonstrated the growing tensions among group members: a local TV station invited Stephen, Koreen, and Jack to appear on a Sunday morning talk show. Stephen agreed to appear only if he was filmed behind a screen, because he hitchhiked frequently and was afraid that his safety would be jeopardized if his face could be identified.

Jack objected, and he didn't mince words. "That reeks of hiding in the closet."

Instead of avoiding exposure, Jack actually urged FREE to court it. To glean maximum impact from the talk show, he suggested that the group notify some two hundred legislators and urge them to tune in. Stephen eventually decided that he would rather bow out of appearing on the show than risk the chance of being recognized by hostile strangers.

Jack and I understood that Stephen was trying to find a halfway point, a comfortable compromise between what he believed and what he dared. He was scared to be totally honest in public. But we felt that his timid approach was part of the problem. We believed that we should aim for absolute and total equality—not some half-baked compromise that would give us second-class status. We deserve the same rights as any straight couple—to hold hands in public, to dance and hug without fear of losing our jobs or being beaten up. To enjoy the benefits of marriage, including tax breaks, inheritance rights, and public acknowledgment that our love is valid. Like Mother and Daddy always told us McConnell kids: we are as good as anybody else. But in the early days of the gay movement, our conviction wasn't always shared—even in the gay community. Lots of gays had been chased into the closet. They'd been intimidated and injured by family, church, and society. Some had paid dearly for acknowledging who they were.

The internal tensions in FREE began to erode the group's effectiveness. And as Jack's face and words were repeatedly splashed across newspapers, other members got irritated. Eventually, the organization became totally absorbed by infighting and resentment. In December, Stephen started calling individual members to persuade them to change FREE's constitution so that it was led by a three-person coordinating committee rather than a single president. The committee would rotate leadership each month. In January, at a crowded, tense meeting, the group decided—by a single vote—to change the constitution to this decentralized structure. Jack opposed the change. He felt that without a strong leader, FREE could not react swiftly to new developments. Although Jack agreed to serve on the first coordinating committee, he was frustrated by the group's now ponderous decision-making process. He began to look for another way to advance gay rights on campus.

In November, Jack's case against the Air Force inched forward. Jack's attorney had finally been granted access to the investigation reports. As Land suspected, there was no conclusive evidence. Land requested another hearing, and it was scheduled for March 24, 1970. Again, Jack traveled to Washington, D.C., for the hearing. About a month later, in April, he finally got the good news: the review board had revoked his general discharge and reinstated the original honorable discharge.

When Jack wrote to thank Land for his fine work on the case, he gave him his "unqualified permission . . . to cite this case, including my name" because he wanted "this case to be of maximum help to anyone suffering from the prejudice against and discrimination of homosexuals by the Government." Jack also wrote that he looked "forward to the day when I will join you as a member of the Bar defending the rights of others similarly harassed."

During Jack's first year in law school, I watched from a distance as he became the dashing leader of the gay rights movement at the University of Minnesota. His brilliant, forceful style produced reverberations around the state and even the country. Now he had concluded his battle with the Air Force with a fine victory. When I read his letter to Land, pledging to devote his talents to the cause of gay rights, I wept—just a few soft tears of joy. I couldn't have been any prouder of my man.

Applying for our marriage license on May 18, 1970. Photograph by
R. Bertrand Heine. Courtesy of the Minnesota Historical Society.

7

The Right to Marry

· · · · · · ·

On the day that Jack enrolled in law school, we both knew that our preparations for marrying were officially under way. Marriage was our pledge to one another, the nucleus of our personal agenda. We knew our love was as meaningful, as beautiful, and as valid as the love of any two people on Earth, and we were determined to have our sacred bond recognized by the country in which we lived. We were serious about this. We were going to marry each other, fully and legally. We weren't second-class citizens. We intended to have all the recognition and benefits that marriage confers.

The first term in law school includes a course in how to do legal research. As Jack learned, this is the cornerstone of all legal work. Always the eager student, he decided to put his newly mastered research skills into action as soon as his finals were completed in December 1969. So off he trotted to the law library.

That evening, I got an unexpected phone call from him. "Michael? Sit down, I have something to tell you."

My heart skipped several beats. Long-distance phone calls were a costly luxury. Was something wrong?

"We're going to get married," he said.

I sighed. "Yes, I know. That's what we promised when we became lovers. That's why you went to law school."

"I mean *now*," Jack said. "Or whenever you want. On your birthday, maybe."

"Don't we need a marriage license first?" I said.

"That's just it," Jack said. "We can get the license. Now. Anytime. All we have to do is apply. It's legal. There is nothing in the Minnesota statutes that mentions gender. We're old enough to get married, and I'm residing in the state. Nothing says you have to be a man and woman to get married."

This was too good to be true. "Are you sure?"

"I read it with my own eyes. In the law library. I Xeroxed the statute; I'll show it to you. I'm telling you, Michael, there's nothing in the statute that says we can't. And if the law doesn't specify that something is prohibited, then it's legal. That's the way it works. There's no regulation in Minnesota that prohibits marriage between two consenting men. So that means we can get married. It's as simple as pie."

Jack wasn't kidding around—I could hear the assurance in his voice. So it was a good thing that I was sitting down. This was stupendous news—I was going to marry the man I loved! We could go get a license whenever we liked. I felt like waltzing.

On my next visit, I quizzed him about the details. He explained that marriage is regulated by the states, not the federal government. Each state decides who can marry and how, and these rules are slightly different from state to state. For instance, in some states, close cousins are eligible to marry, but they may not be eligible in other states.

In Minnesota, the marriage statutes didn't mention gender at all.

"Whatever isn't prohibited by law is permitted," Jack said. "That's the first principle that we learned in law school."

We were cuddling on the couch. "So I can make an honest man of you, Michael McConnell, anytime you want." He winked at me.

I leaned close as if to whisper in his ear, but instead I stuck out my tongue and licked his earlobe. He groaned. I said, "Okay, Plaintiff, you win your case. But first, I'm going to make you beg the courts for mercy." I began unbuttoning his shirt, fumbling deliberately so my fingers slid over his chest and belly.

We decided to apply for our license in the spring. Since my Park College contract would be finished in early summer, we could have our ceremony as soon as I moved to Minneapolis. Of course, we understood that both of us couldn't survive on his G.I. Bill money, so our plans hinged on me getting a job. But I wasn't too worried about that. I had my degree in library science and two years of great on-the-job experience at a respected college. The Twin Cities of Minneapolis and St. Paul are home to the central University of Minnesota campus as well as many smaller colleges. I was confident that I would have a job offer before my Park College contract ran out. Our future together was clicking into place, just as we had dreamed it.

In late March, I interviewed with Ralph Hopp at the University of Minnesota Libraries about a job opening on

the St. Paul campus. After he received my college tran-
scripts and references, we met for a second interview. I
really liked Hopp, and I was pretty sure the feeling was
mutual. A slender man, Hopp was neat in his attire and
calm in his mannerisms. His office was orderly, with sleek,
contemporary-style furniture. It looked both professional
and tasteful—the kind of environment that I aspired to.
Hopp was very interested in my experiences in automa-
tion at Park College and seemed enthusiastic about incor-
porating my knowledge into the University of Minnesota
library system.

A few days later, he wrote and offered me the job. I was
elated! Not only did this mean that I could move to Minneapolis and be with Jack, but the job was also the perfect
step up my career ladder: I would be head of the cataloging division at the St. Paul campus library, with a rank of
instructor and a salary of $11,000. I wrote a letter to Hopp
accepting the position, then told my boss at Park College
that I wouldn't be renewing my contract.

Jack looked over Hopp's letter and concluded that
it was an official job offer. Just to be sure that our marriage wasn't going to rock the boat before we got safely to
shore, he wrote to Hopp as a representative of FREE. He
asked whether Hopp or his managers would do anything
to sanction a gay person in their department for being
open about their sexual preferences. Jack specifically asked
if dancing man-to-man in public would be a problem for
an employee under Hopp's supervision.

Hopp's answer was reasonable and reassuring—just
what I expected from him. He wrote: "Our concern is
with the conduct of Library staff members only when they

are on duty, or . . . when they are representing themselves as Library staff members." He reinforced this position in a private conversation with Jack.

Jack also wrote to his siblings to tell them about our plans. We knew there'd be a burst of publicity when we applied for our marriage license, and Jack thought it would be courteous to give his family an advance warning. But he was not in any mood to apologize for our lifestyle. In a long handwritten letter that he sent to each sister and brother, he said he was giving them a choice: either accept our marriage and welcome us as part of the Baker family or sever any future relationship with their brother.

His favorite sister, Judy, responded. She said she would continue to support and love Jack, as always. But most of his siblings didn't even acknowledge Jack's letter. He was annoyed, but committed to the future that we'd chosen for ourselves. As far as he was concerned, each of them had made a decision and it was final. He would have no further contact with those siblings who objected to the man he was. I would be his family from that day forward, and he would keep in contact with Judy. The rest of his siblings would no longer exist for him.

As for my family—the idea of an actual marriage between two men was radical enough in 1970 to rattle my usually calm mother. Her biggest worry was about my safety and welfare. Although she expressed doubt about whether marriage was a good idea, she trusted me enough to leave the decision to my judgment. (She also knew her Michael well enough to realize that once my mind was made up, she wasn't likely to be able to pressure me into changing it!)

I received this letter from her:

Dearest Mike and Jack,

We got your card, Mike. I pray that what you
are doing is all legal and right and not a big mistake
and that you both will not have a lot of regrets and
will be very happy. However, I thought maybe
things were better like they were. I can't see how
getting married can help any. It's pretty easy to just
walk out of a situation if a misunderstanding occurs
than having a legal procedure.

Honey, we want the best for you and you know
all this. You are your own judge of what you want
out of life. May God in Heaven be your guide.

Love Always,
Your Mother

I didn't expect Mother and Dad to greet the marriage idea
with enthusiasm, but I trusted that they would soon get
used to it.

At last, everything was in place. My birthday is in May,
so we decided that our marriage license would be my
birthday present—the best gift anybody could give me. I
was scheduled to start my new job on July 1. As soon as
I moved to Minneapolis, we would have our ceremony.
It was perfect—I had always dreamed of a summer wedding, surrounded by lush greenery and colorful blossoms.
I could practically inhale the fragrance of the flowers as I
imagined our nuptials.

I took a few days of leave in May so I could be in the
Twin Cities during the workweek when the courthouse
was open for business. On May 18, 1970, Jack and I shaved

and dressed in white shirts, matching ties, and our best dark suits. As we were getting ready, I glanced at our reflections in the bedroom mirror. Both of us looked neat and trim. We were a perfectly matched couple—mirror images of two young men with fine prospects. Suddenly, my face blossomed into a gigantic grin. When I realized that I was beaming like a silly baboon, I forced myself to assume a more serene expression. The last thing that I wanted to do was look like an idiot in front of the reporters' cameras!

And there would be cameras. We didn't know what kind of reception we could expect from the courthouse clerks, so we had decided to alert the press. We arranged for FREE to issue a news release on the day before our license application. It was written by one of the members, Jim Chesebro, and it stated that "any relationship that promotes honesty, self-respect, mutual growth and understanding for two people and which harms no other person should be accepted by the law." With reporters watching the proceedings, we knew the clerks would have to be courteous and respectful to us.

We arrived at the Hennepin County Courthouse at 3 p.m., filled out the license application, and paid our $10. This is how the reporter for the student newspaper, the *Minnesota Daily,* described the scene: "The two men . . . caused only a minor stir as they walked into the marriage license bureau. . . . Slightly embarrassed reporters and photographers fluttered around them while most of the office workers stood in small clusters and tittered."

On the way out of the building, Jack and I held up our hands in a V for victory as we smiled at the knot of reporters. We paused to answer a few of their questions.

Jack told the reporters, "This is not a gimmick." Then we drove off, the sun reflecting off the hood of our car on a glorious afternoon. What a day! (And after we got back to Jack's apartment, what a night!)

It usually takes about six days for an application for a marriage license to be processed. But news about our license came sooner. On the day after we applied, an article in the St. Paul daily newspaper, the *Pioneer Press,* quoted Hennepin County attorney George Scott: "Without getting into the law . . . I'll just say that it's my understanding that there should be a male and female involved."

Instead of issuing our license, Scott issued a seven-page legal opinion. He recommended that our application be denied on the basis of some fine print in the statutes regarding procedures: in order to distribute the task of processing marriage licenses fairly among jurisdictions, the State of Minnesota had specified that a license was to be issued in the county where the woman lives. Scott interpreted this as meaning that "if no woman is involved, a license can't be issued." (Talk about ridiculous—by this reasoning, it would have been perfectly fine for two women to marry.) Scott also cited a 1949 ruling by the Minnesota Supreme Court stating, "It is the duty of the state, in the conservation of public morals, to guard the (marriage) relation."

When a reporter from the Minneapolis daily evening newspaper, the *Star,* contacted him, Scott said, "To permit two males to marry would result in an undermining and destruction of the entire legal concept of our family structure in all areas of law." Good grief! Jack and I certainly believed that our love for each other was momentous, but neither of us would have claimed the extraordinary power to destroy our society's entire family structure by merely saying "I do." The reporter questioned Scott specifically about the lack of any state laws that prevented men from marrying each other, but Scott evaded the question. He said, "The legislature does not intend a result that is absurd, impossible of execution, or unreasonable."

The reporter also contacted Gerald R. Nelson, clerk of district court, Hennepin County, and asked if he would issue the marriage license. Nelson said that he had no intention of doing so.

So much for living in a country governed by laws! I was flabbergasted. If the wording of the law didn't suit the taste of these officials, were they simply going to reinterpret it to mean whatever they wanted?

Jack was furious. "The first principle we learned in law school is that what's not prohibited is permitted," he fumed. "Scott and Nelson may not like the idea of us getting married, but they have no right to prevent it."

We were both frustrated. Although the law didn't give these officials the right to prevent our marriage, Jack and I were learning that reality does not always follow the rules. Many young people were learning the same sad but age-old truth as they marched for civil rights and demanded equal pay for women's work. Scott and Nelson shouldn't have had the right to deny our license, but they were state officials, so they had the power to do whatever they liked. Getting married was not going to be, as Jack had optimistically predicted, "simple as pie."

We had another battle on our hands, this time for the right to marry. It would be the most important battle of our lives.

UNIVERSITY OF MINNESOTA

BOARD OF REGENTS

Faculty, Staff, and Student Affairs Committee

June 22, 1970

MINUTES

A meeting of the Faculty, Staff, and Student Affairs Committee was held in the Regents Room, Morrill Hall, on Monday, June 22, 1970, at 3:30 P.M.

Present: Regent Yngve, presiding; Regents Andersen, Malkerson, and Sherburne; President Moos.

Staff Present: Vice Presidents Smith and Shepherd; Mr. Tierney.

Voted to recommend that the appointment of Mr. J. M. McConnell to the position of Head of the Cataloging Division of the St. Paul Campus Library at the rank of Instructor not be approved.

The Committee adjourned at 5:30 P.M.

R. Joel Tierney, Secretary Pro Tem

8

The Right to Work

· · · · · · · ·

While we consulted with friends in the law school and
Minnesota Civil Liberties Union (MCLU) about how
to pursue our application for a marriage license, we ran
smack-bang into another unexpected roadblock: my job
offer at the University of Minnesota was rescinded.

I was aghast. I knew that approval by the Board of Regents was a part of the university's hiring process, but it
was normally a routine formality. I had an official letter,
complete with a starting date and salary. The letter was
signed by an administrator in the university's library system. How could the Regents *not* approve?

The shocking news came on June 22, 1970, exactly one
month after our marriage license had been denied. (Talk
about a double whammy.) I was informed that the Faculty, Staff, and Student Affairs Committee of the Board of
Regents would be willing to hear a statement from me at
their meeting on July 9. Ironically, that was one week after
I was originally supposed to start work at my new job.

Accompanied by two lawyers from the MCLU, I appeared before the Regents committee. My attorneys did

most of the talking, but I gave a brief statement. The Regents sat, poker-faced, until we finished. There was no back-and-forth. It seemed like we were going through the motions in a scripted play; I didn't think the committee members had any intention of reconsidering their decision. Sure enough, the next morning, the Regents' Executive Committee met in private and recommended that the full board deny my appointment, stating that my "personal conduct, as represented in the public and University news media, is not consistent with the best interest of the University." That afternoon, without further discussion, the full board voted not to approve my appointment. In an interview quoted in the *Minnesota Daily,* the university newspaper, one of the regents, Daniel Gainey, said that hiring me "would enrage ninety percent of the people in the state." He also called me "a damn fool."

This was like a sucker punch. After receiving the university's offer, I had promptly sent in my notice that I was leaving Park College. So I was now living in the Twin Cities without any job prospects. I had my moving expenses to pay, and I had to find some way to support myself as well as to pursue a lawsuit against the university. Because, let me tell you, there was no way that I was going to swallow this kind of blatant discrimination without a fight.

The MCLU offered to represent my case, and we jumped right into battle. We decided we would go through the federal court system, rather than the state courts, because this was about constitutional rights. My case was called *McConnell v. Andersen,* which stands for Michael McConnell against the Board of Regents (Elmer L. Andersen was the chairman of the Board of Regents). On

UNIVERSITY OF *Minnesota*

Office of the Director

UNIVERSITY LIBRARIES
WILSON LIBRARY · MINNEAPOLIS, MINNESOTA 55455

June 25, 1970

Mr. J. Michael McConnell
1139 15th Avenue S. E.
Minneapolis, Minnesota 55414

Dear Mr. McConnell:

In accordance with our telephone conversation on June 25 I am sending you herewith a copy of a letter dated June 24, 1970 from University Attorney R. Joel Tierney in which he informed me of the recommendation of the Faculty, Staff, and Student Affairs Committee of the Board of Regents not to approve your appointment.

As I informed you, under the circumstances you should not begin employment at the University Libraries as you had planned. Also if you wish a hearing before the Committee you may contact Mr. Tierney.

Very truly yours,

Ralph H. Hopp
University Librarian

RHH:jn
cc: 'R. Joel Tierney, University Attorney

Letter from the University of Minnesota, June 1970. Courtesy of the Jean-Nickolaus Tretter Collection in GLBT Studies, University of Minnesota Libraries.

August 5, my attorneys argued in the U.S. District Court before Judge Philip Neville that I had been denied my civil rights. The university's attorney actually admitted that in the ten years that he had held his position it was unprecedented for the Regents to single out and reject one person from a list of candidates to be approved for employment. During his testimony, Regent John Yngve, who chaired the committee that had rejected my appointment, called me a criminal. He said that he "presumed" I had committed sodomy, which was illegal in Minnesota.

Judge Neville extracted the essence of my lawsuit: "What you've got to consider is whether McConnell's activities will actually interfere with his employment." He promised a quick ruling and delivered on his promise: on September 9, he issued a permanent injunction against the university. They had to hire me, as promised, because they had failed to show "an observable and reasonable relationship between efficiency in the job and homosexuality." Neville stated—in what should have been a landmark ruling for gay rights—that I was "as much entitled to the protection and benefits of the laws and due process fair treatment as are others."

Jack and I were jubilant. As soon as we got back to the apartment that we shared with another gay couple, Mike Wetherbee and Jim DeVillier, we started shouting and jumping around. We read sections of Neville's ruling out loud as we cheered and toasted. Wetherbee was also in law school, and he and Jack analyzed the legal language and praised the opinion. It was so clearly stated, so logical. Since it was phrased in language that regular people could understand, how could anyone disagree? A gay man was entitled to the same rights in the workplace as anyone else—that should go without saying. As elementary as the logic was, it was also revolutionary. It meant there was no need to hide in the closet at work, no need to cower with fear. An actual judge had ruled that we had the right to be ourselves on the job as well as behind closed doors.

Since the Regents had been rebuffed in federal court, I thought the case was closed. We could all get on with our lives, and I could start working at the job I had been promised. But no, when you're battling with the powers that be, things are never simple. Two days later, at their regular meeting, the Regents showed their stubborn streak. They instructed their legal counsel "to begin the appeal process."

It was now becoming painfully clear to me that what should have been an easy victory was going to become a protracted, tedious, and costly battle. I couldn't survive on frustration alone, so I took a seasonal job selling clothes at Dayton's department store, and I started working a shift at a gay bar a few nights a week.

I'm a librarian by temperament as well as inclination; I like knowing where things belong and how to place them for easy access and retrieval. Not knowing how long I was going to be involved in the court case, whether I would ever get my university job or not, what was the best course of action—all this uncertainty drove me nuts. I tried not to share my anxieties with Jack, but there were days when I felt like I was going to jump out of my skin. I had to find something meaningful and positive to do with my time. I craved a structure, a purposeful project that would guide my daily activities.

During this difficult period in my life, I began talking with John Preston, one of our friends, about the lack of services for gays in the Twin Cities. John and I started dreaming up a center that would soon become Gay House. Although I didn't get my college degree in social work and never envisioned myself in this type of service work, Gay House became an important part of my life for the next few years. By helping other gays who were coping with pain, disappointment, and crisis, I helped myself weather my own difficulties. Looking back, I count Gay House as one of my life's proudest accomplishments, and I think the story of the creation of Gay House is important enough to merit its own chapter in my personal history.

Meanwhile, I awaited the next scene in my legal drama, and I racked my brain for a way to change the mindset of the Regents. Maybe a public outcry of scholars would convince them that they had made a mistake? My case was fundamentally about intellectual freedom, and that's pretty much the first commandment of any library. So in mid-October 1970, I attended the Minnesota Library Association (MLA) conference in Rochester, Minnesota. Mitch Freeman, the head of technical services for the Hennepin County Library system, introduced a resolution on my behalf. It proposed collecting information about my case and forwarding this to the American Library Association with a request to investigate the hiring practices of the University of Minnesota Libraries.

Although the resolution was heartily approved by the membership, the group's officers were less than enthusiastic. Gil Johnsson, the president, expressed concern about the impact of the resolution on librarians in small towns.

I knew that he considered me an outsider because I had recently moved from Kansas City. Gil announced that it would be my responsibility—not theirs—to file a request for action with the parent organization, the American Library Association (ALA). I left the conference feeling betrayed. It seemed to me that my struggle against job discrimination was part of an important war for intellectual freedom and fair treatment. I shouldn't have had to beg for crumbs of support from my colleagues. They should have stood tall beside me, united and proud.

Even though I had received a mixed message at the MLA conference, I wanted to believe that the ALA would champion my cause. Librarians are, after all, a critical part of any society's culture because we are guardians of our history. Freedom of expression is as basic to our profession as breathing. There was no question that I had been unfairly treated; the district court in Minnesota had acknowledged that the law was on my side. The University of Minnesota was acting the part of a bully and picking on me, and I was a member of the ALA. If the parent organization for librarians ignored such an affront, then none of its members would ever be safe from discrimination.

I didn't plan to give the ALA any excuse to hesitate, so I began to compile my request for action. It became a sixteen-page paper with 127 attachments. I planned to submit this hefty document to the organization's Intellectual Freedom Committee that upcoming January.

John Preston (right) with me at the Minneapolis Civic Center, 1973.

9

Gay House

· · · · · · · · ·

Any account about Gay House has to begin with John
Preston. John was a confident young man who became
my close friend. He had moved to the state around the
same time that I did, and he lived in Minneapolis for about
five years. John and I created Gay House together.

Although I didn't have much time for casual
friendships—what with working two jobs and planning
strategy for our marriage license and my job discrimination lawsuits—John and I got to know each other through
activities sponsored by FREE. We developed an instant
bond. Like me, he was a few years older than most college kids. He had lived in other places; he had already
graduated from college, held a job, and been in serious
relationships—some of them painful. He was out of the
closet and comfortable with his own identity.

John was an easy fellow to like. He was about my
height, slim, with sandy hair and a mustache. Whenever
I remember him, I picture him smiling and laughing. He
had an easygoing manner and the gift of gab—on paper as

well as in person. I've always been drawn to courageous people, and that certainly described John. He left the Twin Cities to become the editor of the *Advocate,* the national gay paper of the time. After leaving that job, he actually earned his living as a hustler in San Francisco for a while. Later, he fearlessly described his experiences in articles and in a successful series of gay erotic novels. Sadly, John contracted AIDS and died at the age of forty-eight.

John had come to Minneapolis because of its reputation for having a strong gay community. But off campus, the only settings where gay people in the Twin Cities could really meet were in the gay bars. I've met my share of men in bars, and while that may be fun and fizzy, it's not the best setting for establishing a relationship. Aside from the pressure for fast sex, it's usually hard to talk above the noise. Bars are generally not conducive places for people to open up and explore deep needs and serious concerns. The truth is, there was a complete void of vital social services for gays living off campus in the Twin Cities in 1970; many gay men and women were coming to the area, and some were in desperate need of help. John and I started talking about how the void could be filled.

Funding would have to be one of our initial concerns, of course, because we would need a physical location where gay men and women could go and interact. That meant paying rent. Of course, the needs of the gay community went beyond mere social interactions. Because of society's condemnation, many gay people needed all kinds of support. I had firsthand knowledge of this since the Board of Regents had denied me my job after they realized that I was an openly gay man. Even though the Twin Cities were considered fairly friendly to gays, John had also faced discrimination when he tried to enroll in a class at Northwestern Lutheran Theological Seminary in St. Paul and was refused admittance.

John and I brainstormed a wish list of services that we'd like to see offered at our center. We both knew gay men who had been rejected by their families and thrust penniless onto the streets. Housing, job counseling, and basic things like food and laundry would have to be provided until these men could get back on their feet. Sometimes people turned to alcohol or drugs or worse to dull their pain. A gay community center would need to provide drug and crisis intervention, including a phone hotline available twenty-four hours a day. John was acutely aware of the need for crisis intervention since his lover in Boston had recently committed suicide. We expected some people to come to Gay House with medical problems; sexually transmitted diseases were rampant among youth in those days, and the gay community shared this problem. And with the cops harassing gay men, people would need legal referrals, too. Gay men and women faced deep self-hatred and religious crises, having so often been cast out by their family and church, so we would also need to offer counseling services.

The list was daunting. Realistically, John and I knew that Gay House would not be able to fill every need—at least, not right away. But once we got the ball rolling, we figured things would fall into place. Gradually, we'd amass a list of medical, legal, and religious services that we could refer people to in the Twin Cities. The important thing was to get started and get visible.

It didn't take us long. John and I started talking about a gay community center as 1970 drew to a close. Jack and Mike Wetherbee helped us draft by-laws and articles of incorporation, and John began the search for funding. He had actually been exploring the idea of entering the seminary when he moved to Minneapolis, and this turned out to be a tremendous asset because he "talked the talk" and he was comfortable approaching church leaders. He started by making contact with churches that provided general social services in the Twin Cities.

As soon as we received a $2,000 seed grant from the Joint Urban Mission Project, we began looking for a location. We found a house in a safe, quiet residential neighborhood, at 216 Ridgewood Avenue in Minneapolis. This was a perfect spot for a drop-in center. It had on-street parking and was near a bus stop, so there was easy access. We knew that a lot of gay people lived in this neighborhood, so visitors to Gay House would have no reason to feel conspicuous, nor would they be likely to get harassed or attacked.

We furnished the center sparsely, with a few second-hand couches and tables. Our idea was to keep the place low-key but inviting. Then we drew up a schedule of volunteers to staff it. A lesbian named Cindy Hanson was our first paid director. Bruce Gardner, a student at the University of Minnesota who would eventually become an Episcopal priest, agreed to live in the house for a few months to ensure that it was never vacant and in no danger of robbery or defacement. We figured that people were

High school graduates: Jack in Des Plaines, Illinois, in 1959, and myself in Norman, Oklahoma, in 1960.

The photographer from Look magazine captured us strolling through campus at the University of Minnesota in 1970. Photograph by Charlotte Brooks.

From the book The Gay Crusaders, *by Kay Tobin and Randy Wicker.*
Photograph by Kay Tobin Lahusen, 1972. Copyright Manuscripts
and Archives Division, The New York Public Library.

American as apple pie! With Jack is Mama D, proprietor of a popular Dinkytown restaurant near the university. This was a poster during Jack's 1971 race for student body president at the University of Minnesota. Photograph by Paul Hagen.

*The Social Responsibilities Round Table–Gay Task Force at the American Library
Association conference, Dallas, Texas, June 1971. Several people who would become
famous in the fight for gay liberation are in this photograph with me and Jack: Steve Wolf
is in the front row on the left, and Barbara Gittings is standing beside Jack. Between Steve
and me, in the back row, is Israel Fishman. Photograph by Kay Tobin Lahusen.*

We were always reviewing legal documents in the early 1970s. Photograph by Charlotte Brooks.

Married!
September 3, 1971.
Photograph by
Paul Hagen.

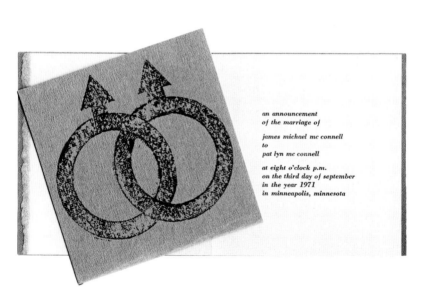

an announcement
of the marriage of

james michael mc connell
to
pat lyn mc connell

at eight o'clock p.m.
on the third day of september
in the year 1971
in minneapolis, minnesota

Our wedding announcement. Courtesy of the Jean-Nickolaus
Tretter Collection in GLBT Studies, University of Minnesota Libraries.

Our marriage certificate.

Our honeymoon—we are wearing the robes that Mother made for us, and Jack is holding the wedding rings that Terry Vanderplas designed. Photograph by Kay Tobin Lahusen, 1971.

Relaxing in our Dinkytown apartment, 1970. Photograph by Charlotte Brooks.

Jack—the engineer, attorney, gay activist, and (best of all) my husband. Photograph by John Hustad, 1972.

*Marching in the 1974 Gay Pride Parade, Minneapolis. Courtesy of the
Jean-Nickolaus Tretter Collection in GLBT Studies, University of Minnesota Libraries.*

During his 1973 race for a seat on the Minneapolis city council, Jack used this image on a billboard in Dinkytown alongside the headline "The Good Life?" It's a parody of a Time *magazine cover that featured Governor Wendell Anderson. Photograph by John Munsell.*

I have always been a librarian by temperament as well as training. Photograph by Peter Denzer, 1978.

Socko was one of the gorgeous cats that graced our lives.
Photograph by Ric Johnson, 1984.

At our home in Minneapolis, with our wonderful coauthor and dear friend Gail Langer Karwoski. Photograph by Melissa Davidson, Studio threesixty5.

more likely to drop in after work or school, so we made sure that volunteers were on hand at key times—in the afternoons, evenings, and into the night. Only gay men and women were counselors and volunteers at Gay House; they were trained by the United Methodist Voluntary Service and the Youth Services Coalition.

In March 1971, Gay House opened its doors. It was one of the first gay community centers in the country. Just as Minneapolis had been a pioneer when FREE, one of the first gay student organizations, was formed on campus, the city was again on the leading edge of the burgeoning gay liberation movement with the establishment of Gay House.

To let people know about Gay House, the staff members printed up flyers. Volunteers distributed them in the gay bars, on campus, and around the city. One of our typical flyers read:

> Gay?—or think you might be?
> You've got friends. Gay House provides
> Gay help for Gay people by Gay people. . . .
> If you've got a hassle or would just like
> to rap, give us a call. . . .
> Love and let Love.

Gay House offered a full schedule of events, seven nights a week. Political action meetings were held often, as well as many other activities: yoga and sewing classes; card games, chess and checkers nights; tennis and softball games; movie nights; informal "rap" (discussion) nights; and counselor-led addiction group sessions. People were encouraged to drop by, as they wished or needed, for an informal chat or a scheduled event.

Once the center was up and running, I agreed to serve on its board of directors to oversee operations. Given my work schedule, I knew I didn't have time to be a regular volunteer or take part in the center's everyday operations, but I stopped by whenever I could. I was glad to lend a hand, and I enjoyed the atmosphere of the place.

I never knew what to expect when I did stop by. I remember one afternoon, I parked in front and found a kid—he looked to be about the age of a college student—on the steps. He nearly jumped out of his skin as I walked up the path. I said hello. He didn't answer, and the expression on his face told me loud and clear that he was in trouble. I figured that he was probably tripping on some drug. I recognized the frozen glare of paranoia in his eyes and the tension in his neck muscles.

I spoke again, keeping my voice soothing and gentle. "I'm Mike," I told him. "I help out here at Gay House. Do you want to go inside?"

He didn't answer so I asked if I could sit by him. He nodded vaguely, and I sat on the steps. Gradually, I started talking. I don't remember what I said, but I knew my words were less important than the tone of my voice. The kid needed reassurance. He needed to come back from whatever terrible place he was in. He needed to feel grounded on good, solid earth. When he began to calm down, I asked if he'd like to stretch out on the grass. I knew he needed to feel that he wasn't alone, that there were people who cared about him. I massaged his chest until his muscles relaxed. When I could see that his breathing was slow and even, I invited him inside again. He stood and gave me a shy grin. I took him inside and introduced him to one of the trained staff members.

Another day, I walked in and found everybody in a flurry about a plainclothes man who had been seated in a car outside all day.

"I bet he's FBI," someone said. "I'm pretty sure I've seen him out there before. He's spying on us. Casing out the place."

I had no idea whether the rumor had any truth to it, but I decided to take a bold approach and confront the fellow. So I strode out the door, up to the car, and greeted the clean-shaven man behind the steering wheel. I told him that my name was Mike and offered to shake hands.

"Would you like to come in?" I asked. "I'll be glad to give you a tour of the place if you're interested."

The man smiled at me but shook his head. "No, that's okay."

He promptly started the car and drove away. Although there were plenty of rumors, we never knew for certain if the FBI or the police had made any attempt to monitor our activities.

Usually, it was a board meeting that brought me to Gay House. But I always tried to leave myself some extra time to visit folks while I was there. Whenever I stopped by, there were people sitting around on the couches, talking. It was a good place to be, a casual, nonjudgmental atmosphere. Although I was there to help, organize, and counsel, I took strength from the sense of community. This was an anxious period for me. I had my own demons to wrestle in the courts and the job market. Gay House provided me with the same good vibes that it offered thousands of others. I knew I was in a safe, warm place and that I was surrounded by genuine people who cared.

One young fellow, a college student from Ames, Iowa, named Dennis Brumm, drove all the way to Minneapolis to visit the center. He wrote a funny and poignant account of his experience and decades later posted it on his website, where I happened on it. Dennis discovered Gay House through a letter from Jack. After he'd read an article about an openly gay man winning the U of M student body presidency, Dennis wrote to Jack, and he was astonished when Jack answered his letter. Jack suggested that isolation was part of the oppression of gay men and invited Dennis to visit Gay House. It took all of Dennis's courage to make that trip, but I'm fairly certain that it changed his life. Here's a peek at how Dennis remembers his experience from the longer account on his website:

> Although the drive was uneventful, I could have been certified as being officially Beyond Nervous Wreck by the American Psychiatric Association, as I arrived in Minneapolis.
>
> I found the Gay House; the directions were easy. I parked my car several blocks away so nobody would know I was associated with my car and this house or that my car was associated with me and that house, or whatever it was that I was being paranoid about which was really just about being alive and in the vicinity of known "homosexuals." It sounds so silly now, but it was exactly what I felt at my young isolated age of 19. . . .

But I couldn't walk in.

I could not even cross the street to Gay House. I was so close but I might as well have been in Iowa. I was frozen in place standing my ground across the way and the street between me and the house became more than a street; it was a moat. . . . I can still distinctly see the face of this mentor who talked me through the fear that night. He was probably in his 30s, which seemed ancient to me then. It was a kind face, and he was understanding and told me everyone who is gay goes through things very much like I was, and he told me I wasn't alone, and that it was generally harder for people who came from rural areas. I couldn't believe how reassuring it was to hear what I was hearing, and I wanted to believe it so badly. I was not the sole miserable creature of my ilk I'd feared I was. . . .

Gay House wasn't an unusual building. . . . There was a stairway straight ahead when you went in the front door and to the left a living room filled with people. Rather I should now say the living room was filled with gay people. They accepted me as just another gay man. I was no longer a sole "homosexual" drifting along alone. It was no big deal I'd come into the house and very soon I felt I belonged somewhere. Within minutes a sense of calm came over me I didn't really expect to feel the rest of my life.

There may really be only a few specific days in anyone's life that really shape the future of who a person will be; normally our days blur into a wad

of cosmic insignificance. . . . Then there are those
days like that October evening was in Minneapolis
in 1971 for me.

Over the next five years, Gay House forged connec-
tions with a variety of agencies in the Twin Cities and
beyond: the Youth Services Coalition, Hennepin County
Social Services and Hennepin County Medical Center,
Lutheran Social Services, Vietnam Veterans Against the
War, and the Red Door Clinic, to name a few. Our volunteers referred people to these agencies for specialized
services. The center also relocated twice. Eventually, the
many services offered by Gay House split into a network
of social services that included Gay Community Services
and the Lesbian Resource Center. Gay House remained
one feature of this network; it was geared explicitly as a
drop-in center for the younger and counterculture com-
ponent of the gay community.

While I remained closely connected with Gay House
for its first few years, I gradually let go of my leadership
role on the board and moved on to other activities. Jack
and I were doing a lot of public speaking by then. In 1973,
I got a job in a public library, and I became absorbed in
my work. Jack and I began playing an active role in city
politics.

Unfortunately, Gay House came to a sad ending when
a scandal involving its last director tarnished the center's
reputation, and by 1980, the center was shut down. But
during nearly a decade of operation, Gay House was a life-
altering force—if not a lifesaver—for many of the young

people who found their way through its doors. I'm very proud of the work the center did. I think of Gay House as a tribute to my brave friend, John Preston. It's a source of satisfaction for me that such a fine thing grew from the misery of the darkest period of my life, when I was engaged in my lonely struggle for the basic human right to do the job that I was trained to do.

The Homosexual Couple

As far as Jack Baker and Michael McConnell are concerned, their relationship "is just like being married."

BY JACK STAR   PHOTOGRAPHS BY CHARLOTTE BROOKS

Jack Baker and Michael McConnell, both 28, are homosexuals. They share a flat with another male couple in a shabby Minneapolis neighborhood near the University of Minnesota, where Baker is a second-year law student. "As far as Jack and I are concerned," says McConnell, "our relationship is just like being married."

Sex researchers are beginning to realize that homosexual behavior can be as varied as heterosexual conduct.

Not all homosexual life is a series of one-night stands in bathhouses, public toilets or gay bars (those queer, mirror images of the swinging-singles straight scene). Some homosexuals—a minority—live together in stable, often long-lasting relationships, like Baker's and McConnell's.

"We met at a 'barn party' at the University of Oklahoma where I was a student," says McConnell. "In June, 1967, we moved in together." McCon-

nell comes from Norman, home of the University of Oklahoma. His father is a barber there. McConnell had declared himself a homosexual at 19, "although I knew for years before exactly what I was." A pharmacy student for four years, he switched to the library school because of his first lover, a librarian with whom he had lived for five years. McConnell now has a masters in library science.

"My mother couldn't care less what I am," says McConnell. "She has another son, three daughters and nine grandchildren. She tells me: 'You're our son and we love you. We only hope you'll be happy.' My parents kiss and hug Jack like they do me."

Baker experienced a more difficult life. He was the youngest of ten children; his mother died when he was five, and his father, a year later. He grew up with a brother and two sisters in a Catholic boarding school just outside Chicago. There, Baker had fleeting homosexual experiences. In college, he interrupted his studies to serve four years in the Air Force and received a degree in industrial engineering from the University of Oklahoma; later he got a masters in business administration from Oklahoma City University.

"The only thing a homosexual owes his family is to keep them from learn-

Jack Baker (top left) and Michael McConnell have been living together for over three years. Last May (above), they applied for a marriage license but Minnesota authorities won't issue one.

ing the truth via the grapevine, through gossip," says Baker. "I have lived this life secretly for 15 years, and I'm tired of being a hypocrite. On Thanksgiving Day, 1969, I assembled my eight living brothers and sisters and told them. My eldest brother took it badly—he said he never wanted me in his house again—but thank God I told them. You have an obligation to live life as you see fit."

Baker's strong feelings brought him notoriety and some grief. Last year, after moving to Minneapolis to go to law school on the GI Bill, he got the idea of applying with McConnell for a marriage license. This, he says,
continued

Our profile in Look *magazine, January 26, 1971. Courtesy of the Jean-Nickolaus Tretter Collection in GLBT Studies, University of Minnesota Libraries.*

10

New Year, Lots of Resolutions

· · · · · · · · · ·

As the year 1970 came to a close, we were embroiled in preparations for our most important battle: the right to validate our love through a legal marriage. Even back then, we understood the magnitude of what we were trying to do. Marriage is the central goal of the gay rights movement; being gay is about who you love, and marriage is the way that we declare and validate love in our society. With the right to marry, we could take our place as full citizens of our world. Without this right, we would be relegated to either the closet or the back of the bus.

As soon as our Hennepin County marriage license was rejected in May, we started thinking of ideas about how to proceed. Jack read related law cases, prepared briefs, and constructed timelines. Mike Wetherbee agreed to act as our attorney. He was a year ahead of Jack in law school, and now that he had graduated he was able to practice law. We trusted Mike. He had been an active and dynamic member of FREE; he negotiated with the university administration to allow the first gay dances on campus. Since we shared our apartment with him and his lover, we knew we would have plenty of time and privacy to mull over our case.

Like Jack, Mike had a brilliant legal mind. He was creative, insightful, and energetic. A likable fellow, he was a great conversationalist, and his favorite topic was the law. Mike was about the same height as me. He reminded me of a handsome but gangly puppy that has reached its full height but not yet bulked up to adult weight. Jack had watched him work a courtroom, and he liked what he had seen. Mike's professional demeanor was amiable, and his preparation was thorough. There was nothing obnoxious about him, nothing to offend a judge or jury.

On October 29, Mike tried a legal tactic to force the clerk of court to issue our marriage license. He filed for a writ of mandamus in Hennepin County District Court. A writ of mandamus is a court-ordered command that forces someone (in this case, officials in Hennepin County) to do what is required by law. If the district court judge would agree to this, then our case would be finished and Hennepin County would be required to issue our marriage license. No further legal action would be necessary. By ruling in our favor for a writ of mandamus, the district court would, in effect, be saying that yes, we were legally entitled to a marriage license. It would be a swift and definitive way to get what we wanted.

But Mike was new to the legal profession, and he made a procedural error when he filed the writ; he did not inform the state attorney general—as required by statute—that among our arguments we would be raising a federal constitutional issue. After reviewing our case, Judge Stanley K. Kane dismissed it "without prejudice" to the constitutional portion of our claim. Kane's wording meant that he was ruling not on our constitutional argument, only on whether the state's statutes gave us the right to marry. In his ruling, Judge Kane concluded that the marriage statute did not allow two men to marry each other: "It must be concluded that the legislature did not intend to authorize or permit such marriages."

To tell the truth, I've got to admit that I felt a bit of satisfaction from Judge Kane's remarks about our case. He actually said in court that our case had no legal precedents—that, in fact, it broke new ground. I took that as a compliment.

"Well, this judge isn't so bad," I told Jack when we were all discussing the ruling.

He looked at me, puzzled.

"He said our marriage was unprecedented, didn't he? That's a huge compliment. He as much as admitted that we think outside the box." I grinned. "Unlike some of these petty little state officials whose brains are locked in dark, moldy coffins."

Mike's mistake cost us a little time, since he had to file a second motion for a writ of mandamus. He did this in December, this time notifying the attorney general that we were challenging a state statute on the grounds that our constitutional rights had been violated. Since the marriage statute did not specify gender, the county officials shouldn't have had the power to deny us our license—we had a constitutional right to fair treatment under the law.

District Court Judge Tom Bergin heard this motion in January and denied it without comment.

We were not surprised. If either of the district court

judges had ruled in our favor, of course we would have been elated. But we weren't expecting any such easy, direct conclusion. In fact, Jack and Mike had already decided what our next legal action would be once we received an unfavorable ruling on the writ of mandamus. We were following a predictable legal path, from local and state courts to higher courts. In the 1970s, an interpretation of the federal constitution by a state court was entitled to automatic review by the high court. (This is no longer true. Today, the U.S. Supreme Court reviews cases by invitation only.) If the local and state courts denied our motions, we knew we could place our case in front of a court that ruled the entire nation. That was a heady thought—one ruling at a national level would throw open the door for every gay couple in the country.

Bergin's denial meant that we would move to the next step. So we began the appeal of our federal constitutional claim to the Minnesota Supreme Court. In the courts, our case was called *Baker v. Nelson,* which stands for Jack Baker against Gerald Nelson. Nelson was the clerk of the Hennepin County District Court, the official who granted marriage licenses.

In the first month of 1971, two stunning stories catapulted our struggle into national headlines. On January 26, the *Minnesota Daily* announced that Jack was running for student body president at the University of Minnesota. This was huge—never before had an openly gay person announced a run for student body president. On the same day, *Look* magazine's special issue on the American family hit the newsstands. It featured a three-page spread about us, "The Homosexual Couple."

Jack and I knew the *Look* article was coming since the reporter and photographer had visited us during the autumn. What we didn't know was the impact that it would have. The magazine had a circulation of 6.5 million— among the large-format, general interest magazines of the day, its circulation was second only to *Life*.

The *Look* story opened with a full-page black-and-white close-up of our faces as we leaned against a tree. The texture of the bark provided an artful contrast with our clean-shaven, boyishly smooth cheeks. Other black-and-white photographs accompanied the text: They showed us shaving together, cuddling as we relaxed with friends, being sworn in at the courthouse when we applied for our marriage license, and chatting with the priest at the university's Catholic center. The text summarized our unusual legal struggles and provided a glimpse into our very usual domestic life. If it weren't for the fact that we were two men, a reader would almost certainly react with "So what?" We were shown as a young couple, bright with promise, living and loving together.

The reaction to the *Look* article was staggering. We got a flood of letters from all over the United States as well as from foreign countries. Most of the letters were from gay men who were electrified by what we were doing. Many were curious about how we had managed to create a healthy, steady relationship while living in a society that viewed us as a plague. Some of the letters were poignant— the writers told us of their isolation, their yearning for companionship and understanding, their fear of public exposure or their rejection by family members when their homosexuality was found out.

from Louisiana—

Dear Jack & Mike,
   I read the article in *Look* concerning you
both. . . . I was deeply impressed by the article.
I suppose the reason it touched me so was
because I knew I was the same as you. The only
difference is I am, or was, ashamed of it.
   I am twenty and I have known *this* as long as
I can remember, that I *was different*. I have had
to live a lie for so long, at times I almost have a
nervous breakdown. When I saw your pictures I
wished so badly that *I* had someone to share my
love and not be ashamed or try to hide it.

from Georgia—

Dear Jack,
   I am writing you as I'm sure lots of people have.
I live in a small north Georgia town and so far,
evidently, have not come in contact with anyone
who is homosexual towards me. Could you *please,*
if possible, suggest some way of contacting someone or something. The loneliness and depression
are getting to me.

from Michigan—

Dear Sir,
   Please excuse me for bothering you like this,
but I am so mixed up and don't know what to do.

. . . I am 19 years old and currently going to
college. I was engaged to be married but finally
faced the fact that I wasn't happy pursuing that
kind of life. I have had sex with my fiancee many
times and each time I found it more and more
repulsive.

from Arizona—

Dear Jack Baker,
. . . I am gay, but I don't hardly know very
many gay friends. I guess I'm a closet case, as I've
heard some refer to those who have to hide themselves. It's so hard to live what you feel & want to
live when living in a strict & religious family. . . .
In all of the photos in the mag you & Michael
look so happy & content being with each other.
How did you have the nerve to ever show your
feeling by touching, necking, etc., in public?

from North Carolina—

Dear Jack and Michael:
I have just finished reading your story in
'Look.' . . . I admire you very much—your honesty and your courage in doing what you believe
is right. It's too bad that more of us, including me,
can't have the courage to announce ourselves to
the world and then begin to live a completely honest life. But I guess some of us will never have that
kind of courage. . . . I suppose I'm just a little bit

envious of you. I don't care what anybody says or denies, every gay person, deep down, is searching for the type of relationship you have.

from Delaware—

Dear Jack and Mike,
     What can I say? It's only been a matter of hours since the magazine arrived, and I feel like I've known you both for a long time. I don't think I can really express all that it's done to me, and for me, but I'll try. I was moved by the depth, integrity, and beauty of your relationship. It made me face myself and realize what a hypocrite I've been for such a long time. It made me stop and think about who I am, where I am, and where I'm going. Most of all it made me realize how far I've got to go. I'm writing this letter to ask you if you would help me.

Every time we received a letter from someone awash in misery, we took the time to answer it. We knew our encouragement could help those suffering in solitude. Several of the letter writers said that our marriage was a life-changing event for them because it gave them hope.
     Reading these letters made a big impact on me. I understood, more than ever, the value of outreach services for gay men and women. John Preston and I were in the midst of building the network of off-campus services that we had named Gay House. The letters reinforced the importance of our efforts.

After the *Look* article appeared, the bags of mail arrived and kept arriving. There was some hate mail, of course, but such letters were surprisingly few. Instead, almost all the writers wished us well. With that single magazine portrait, it seemed that we'd become one of the nation's closely watched couples. It was hugely reinforcing: We had taken a risk to declare our love openly. We knew we were putting our job prospects and quite possibly our safety on the line. The immediate and heartfelt response from hundreds of people bolstered our personal determination to live openly and honestly. These letters meant so much to us that we have carefully preserved every one of them, as well as copies of the responses that we sent to the writers. (All of this correspondence, as well as news clippings and our other records, are now on file at the Jean-Nickolaus Tretter Collection in GLBT Studies. This wonderful archive is housed—somewhat ironically—on the campus of the U of M.)

Jack's announcement that he was making a run for student body president also produced shock waves. I don't think that many people outside our closest circle of friends realized that he was going to do this, but it really shouldn't have come as a surprise. Several of us had been talking about what should be our next step in the burgeoning gay rights movement. By the start of 1971, it was very clear to us that the movement had outgrown FREE. One year earlier, when FREE had voted to decentralize its governing structure, infighting had begun to hobble the organization. Every meeting, every initiative was stalled in a mire of arguments. To put it bluntly, petty jealousies were sapping the group's effectiveness.

In October 1970, FREE had attempted to host a national convention where gay rights groups from around the country could learn and share strategies. The university refused to let the conference take place in campus facilities—citing my ongoing job discrimination case as the reason—so the meetings were scheduled in Dania Hall on the West Bank. Around 150 gay rights advocates registered, from as far away as New York, Washington, D.C., and San Francisco, as well as from Chicago, Kansas City, and throughout the Midwest. The scheduled speakers included representatives from the Human Rights Commission, the police department, and university faculty.

After all the planning, the conference dissolved into bitter arguments at its opening meeting. Attendees shouted at each other, flinging accusations of racism and sexism. Most of the women walked out to form a separate lesbian caucus. Strident voices insisted that all non-gay speakers be removed from the agenda, and when this initiative passed by a single vote, almost a third of the attendees got up and went home. The remainder turned the conference into a rap session dominated by the loudest voices. Jack and I were plenty disgusted. Such a waste of time and energy.

That gay rights conference proved to us that FREE was no longer an effective vehicle for change. All the internal bickering was just too significant a drain on resources. Largely through Jack's dynamic leadership as president of FREE, midwesterners had become fully engaged in what had become a national debate. With this public awareness in place, we felt the time was critical. We needed to move forward swiftly and boldly to build on our hard-won momentum.

And for us personally, we knew we had to make a tough decision about where we were going to invest our energies. Jack and I were already embroiled in lawsuits about our marriage license and my job. His law school classes had become more intense as he neared graduation. We were barraged by invitations to speak on panels and at focus groups, and this continuing public education—one bible study meeting, one synagogue Hadassah group, one college sociology class at a time—was important. I was scrabbling to support myself after the university squashed my library career, and I was devoting as much time as I could scrape together to Gay House.

We came to the conclusion that Jack needed a larger arena for the quest for gay rights than FREE, and student government seemed the perfect podium.

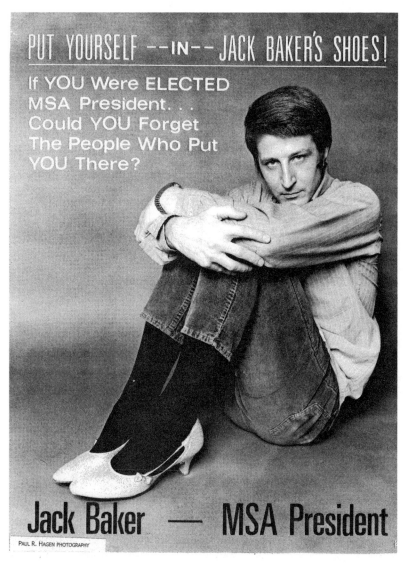

Jack's infamous shoes poster, 1971. Photograph by Paul Hagen.

11

Mister President

• • • • • • • • • •

In January 1971, during his very first interview as candidate
for student body president, Jack established his memorable
style as a campaigner. He insisted that he was not running
as "the gay candidate" as he spoke to the reporter from
the *Minnesota Daily*. He also made a cocky comparison—
designed to raise eyebrows—likening his candidacy to that
of the ever-popular U.S. president John F. Kennedy: Jack
said that when JFK entered the race, "Everyone said that
they would never elect a Catholic." And Jack predicted
(with more optimism than he actually felt) that his being
gay wouldn't deter the students at the university from vot-
ing for him, either.

With Jack in the running, there was a lot more at stake
in this student election than a typical campus race. If he
became president of the University of Minnesota's student
body, Jack would make history. Never before had a university in the United States—or anywhere else, for that
matter—elected an openly gay student. The University of
Minnesota had an enrollment of forty-three thousand students at its Twin Cities campus; it was certainly a major

university, and it was in a major metropolitan area. In 1971, very few people were openly gay the way that Jack Baker was. Because his name and face had been splashed all over the media, millions of people identified him as a gay man. If the students voted him in, they would be sending a clear and revolutionary message: it was okay to be gay.

At the University of Minnesota, campus elections were usually underwhelming events, remarkable chiefly for the lack of voter turnout and interest. Before Jack added himself to the list of candidates, few thought much of the upcoming race. That's why Jack said his campaign would be a good thing, no matter the outcome. If the only thing his candidacy managed to produce was a heterosexual backlash, at least that would be better than apathy.

Along with Jack, nine others registered as candidates for student body president. In keeping with procedure, a group of student senators, the Minnesota Student Association (MSA) Forum, selected three of these—including Jack—to run in the general election. I think the students really started paying attention when Jack was selected by the senators. His candidacy made the campaign a novelty. The campus felt energized—if the students elected Jack, they would be sending the message that the status quo no longer had a stranglehold on their thoughts and actions.

In addition to Jack, the MSA Forum chose a student named Peter Hames, who had a long involvement in various campus political organizations. Hames was expected to be the top vote getter because of his experience with campus politics. The third candidate selected ran as a conservative; he was a member of the campus Republican association.

Once he was in the race, Jack had no intention of making a token run. He offered a platform based on student and minority rights. In the position statement that he submitted when he filed his candidacy, he called for students to take an active role in policy decisions by serving as "bona fide members of all committees of the Board of Regents." He also advocated equal roles for women and blacks on and off campus. And he challenged the university to improve its environmental record by transforming the Mississippi riverfront into a recreation area. If Jack was going to devote his energies to the race, he meant to use it as a forum to promote meaningful change.

Before the campaign got under way, Jack had already earned plenty of name and face recognition. During the race, his posters became the key element in his success. There were three, each designed and shot by a local gay photographer, Paul Hagen. Only one was standard-issue campaign material. The other two were memorable and hilarious.

We dubbed the most remarkable of them the "shoes poster." It was a photograph of Jack wearing a button-down shirt, slim jeans, and dark socks and sitting on the floor with his arms around his knees. Although Jack's grooming and attire suggest a respectable, clean-cut, handsome man—the sort of man that every mom would want her daughter to marry—his shoes are in the forefront. And his shoes are high heels. In large letters across the top of the poster were the words: PUT YOURSELF IN JACK BAKER'S SHOES!

Just as a bit of insider trivia, let me tell you, it wasn't easy to find a pair of women's heels big enough for Jack to cram his feet into for the photograph. We finally managed to locate a pair of heels that belonged to Bob Halfhill, a cross-dresser who was FREE's treasurer. The shoes were hilarious, all by themselves. They were white with tiny, prissy bows—exactly like the shoes that your grandmother might wear to church.

During Jack's campaign, we couldn't keep those posters on campus kiosks and dorm walls. We printed them by the dozens, but as soon as we tacked them up, they went missing.

"Who do you think is tearing them down?" I asked Jack.

He shrugged, "Who knows? Lots of straight men can't stand the sight of anyone who looks different from them."

"I bet they're jealous," I said, smirking. "They only wish their girlfriends looked as sexy as you in heels!"

Jack winked at me.

One day, I actually spotted a student pulling a poster off the wall in a dorm. "Hey, what do you think you're doing?" I hollered. "I just put that up."

The kid looked at me. "I was going to put it in my room."

I was dumbfounded. "Why?"

"Everybody wants them," he said. "They're like a collector's item. You know—a camp classic."

"Okay, here," I said, grinning. I handed him a fresh poster. "Take this one instead. It doesn't have any stapler marks on it."

The shoes poster was such an eye-catcher that it was even reprinted in the *Advocate,* the national gay publication. In fact, years after the campaign, friends often asked us if we had any extra copies that they could frame.

The shoes poster got the most attention, but Jack's other campy poster also stirred up media attention in newspapers around the country, including the *Miami Herald* and the *San Francisco Examiner.* It showed Jack dressed all in white, with his right arm around a matronly woman holding a baby in her arms. On campus, everyone recognized the woman as Mama D, the owner of a popular pizza hangout. Jack and Mama D stood in front of an American flag and a portrait of Lincoln. Jack had a Bible tucked under his left arm, and he held an apple pie. The words that framed the photograph read: "Jack Baker Comes Out—for Things That Count!"

In addition to his posters, Jack's campaign was bolstered by an endorsement by the *Minnesota Daily* on the day before the election: "We believe, quite simply, that Jack Baker is the most qualified and capable candidate. . . . We feel that he has proven and will prove a courageous advocate of social change. . . . We give him our endorsement and strongly urge his election."

The election was a resounding affirmation for Jack. A record turnout of over 6,000 students voted, and Jack won, taking 2,766 votes. Hames received 1,873; the conservative candidate took 1,005; and there were a few hundred write-ins. Jack had done it—he was the first openly gay student body president in the world.

Jack's win was trumpeted all over campus and beyond. On April 8, 1971, Americans across the country heard the stunning announcement on CBS-TV when the legendary Walter Cronkite reported Jack's election on the evening news. The campus newspaper described Jack in what were—back in that era of radical demonstrations—

glowing terms: "a frequent thorn in the side of the Board of Regents and the administration." Newspapers in Atlanta, Miami, Philadelphia, and other major cities, as well as national magazines, carried the story. His election made the *Washington Post,* the *New York Times, Playboy,* and *Time* magazine.

Of all the coverage, my favorite was an article that appeared in the *Advocate* in May. The headline read: "New president greeted by 'so what.'" It ran with the subhead, "He still does the dishes!" That was from one of my quotes: "He may be student body president, but he still has to do the dishes around here."

The same article quoted a seventeen-year-old co-ed on campus: "As long as he stands for the right things, is a good candidate, I don't think somebody's private life should be anybody else's concern."

That teenage girl really got it. She said what so many supposedly mature adults at the university and beyond had missed. Yes, Jack was a gay man. He was also smart, forceful, and goal oriented—qualities that any leader needs. The students understood that he was the best man for the job and that's why they elected him. Back then, I wouldn't have believed that it would take decades for most of America to arrive at the same logical conclusion.

As student body president, Jack lived up to his promises. His performance even earned him the grudging respect of university officials. In September of his first year in office, he got a nod of approval from both university administrators and members of the Board of Regents. While speaking at a press conference that was reported in the *St. Paul Pioneer Press,* President Malcolm Moos acknowledged that he respected Jack's ability to lobby for student interests and admired the presentations that he'd made before administrators.

John Yngve, who was one of the Regents who had spoken publicly against hiring me, admitted that the board had been impressed with Jack's "excellent and rational presentations" at their meetings. "I feel he performs very well under difficult circumstances," Yngve said.

And Paul Cashman, vice president for student affairs, went so far as to say that "Jack is an excellent administrator, is extremely thoughtful and cooperative, has worked with my staff in a whole host of ways and is a highly effective leader. Period."

Double wow—look beyond the label and the world will see the person. Despite our ongoing struggles to claim our legal rights in marriage and on the job, these comments about Jack's performance infused me with hope. I had always known that we were as good as anybody else, and now Jack's highly visible presence was proving this to the world.

MANKATO

Vol. 85 No. 116   28 pages   4 sections

FREE PRESS

Monday, Aug. 16, 1971   Mankato-North Mankato, Minn. 56001   15¢

Daily Record

Births

HILLTOP HOSPITAL UNIT
Girl:
Mr. and Mrs. Thomas Curtis, Route 4, Saturday.
Boys:
Mr. and Mrs. James Sturgeon, 1609 Fifth Ave., today.
Mr. and Mrs. Leon Metz, Cleveland, today.
Mr. and Mrs. Timothy Miller, 149 Lime Valley Lane, Saturday.
Mr. and Mrs. Gary Reichel, 1527 Colony Court, Saturday.
Mr. and Mrs. Kenneth Marshall, Mapleton, Saturday.

Marriages

James M. McConnell, Norman, Okla., and Pat Lynn McConnell, 107 Parkway Ave.
John R. Radick, Fulda, and Jeanette Elling, 703 Carney Ave.
Duane Oftedahl, Pemberton, and Kathleen M. Hansen, 816 N. Sixth St.

Fire Calls

10:23 a.m. Sunday, call to 500 block of Plum Street where auto owned by Melvin Warnke caught fire when a flooded carburetor spilled gas that ignited, causing slight damage to wiring and vacuum hoses.
7:52 p.m. Saturday, call to 500 block of S. Front St., where gasoline had leaked from tank of car owned by William Scofield, Hibbing.
2:45 p.m. Saturday, call to 204 Iota Ave., owned by Dr. Vasile Posteuca. Unattended cooking had melted bottom out of pan on stove. Fire was out on arrival; no damage.

COUNTY COURT

DISORDERLY CONDUCT — James Weingartz, 19, 820 Lyndale; 20 days in jail suspended on following conditions: no further law violations, good behavior, report to Minnesota Valley Mental Health Center and follow any course of treatment prescribed.
DRIVING AFTER SUSPENSION — Ronald Wilder, Mankato, 30 days suspended, paid $75 fine.
CARELESS DRIVING — Robert Hanson, 19, Wells, paid $30; Valeria Muetzel, 315 Franklin, paid $30.
OVER SINGLE AXLE WEIGHT — Dwight Yaeger, 613 W. 2nd; $85, one-half suspended.

Weather

Mankato Weather the Past 48 Hours to 7 A.M. Monday:
Maximum: 81
Minimum: 55
River: 2.50'
Sunrise: 6:15
Sunset: 8:17
Saturday, Aug. 14:
Maximum: 77
Minimum: 52
River: 2.55'
Forecast Southern Minnesota:
Fair to partly cloudy and a little warmer through Tuesday: low tonight 55-63; high Tuesday 86-92.

The announcement of our marriage license (with "Lyn" misspelled)
in the Mankato Free Press, August 16, 1971. Courtesy of the Jean-Nickolaus Tretter
Collection in GLBT Studies, University of Minnesota Libraries.

12

Short Trip to Blue Earth

· · · · · · · · · · · ·

Our lives were jam-packed in the early seventies. It's hard, looking back, to separate each strand and move chronologically through events. While we were campaigning for Jack's student body presidency, we were involved in court battles for our license to marry. At the same time, I was pursuing legal action against the Regents to get my university job. All the while, Jack continued to study for his classes at the law school, and I earned what income I could get from part-time jobs while rushing off to organizational meetings at Gay House. Despite all these separate demands on our time and attention, the central fiber in our story was our desire to marry. The breakthrough that finally made this possible can be traced to a seemingly innocent conversation in 1970.

"You know," Jack said to me one evening out of the clear blue, "adoption gives you about 90 percent of the benefits of marriage."

I looked at him. Of course I recognized that he had something up his sleeve. This was his way of challenging me to fish for it.

"And your point is?" I asked, as I plunked our plates on the table and slid into my chair. "I've already got a mother and daddy, and I happen to like them just fine."

Jack puffed out his lips in a mock pout. "But what about me? I'm just a poor little orphan boy. Won't you take me under your wing?"

I rolled my eyes as I unrolled my napkin. "And why is it that I'd want to adopt you, Jack? It's not like you're a little helpless kid—you're all grown up. As a matter of fact, we're the same age. And it's not like I'm piling up a big estate here by working part-time jobs. What would be the point of making you my heir?"

"Well, let's say one of us was in a bad wreck and ended up in a coma in the hospital. If we were next of kin, they would have to consult us about any major medical decisions for each other," he said. "And on a more pleasant note, we'd be entitled to tax breaks because we could file as a family."

This was starting to make some sense. "Okay, I'm listening. Keep going," I said.

"And just remember, we're not going to be poor forever," Jack said. "Librarians may not earn a fortune, but one of us *is* getting his law degree *on top* of his engineering and business degrees. I'd say that *he* could probably expect to earn a pretty good salary, someday—enough for a nice house and a flashy car and a fat bank account. Wouldn't you like to be that person's next of kin?"

I pointed out that we were already devoting a great deal of money and energies to the lawsuit to get our marriage license. Not to mention all the time we were pouring into my lawsuit to get my job back. Our resources were already stretched thin.

"Do you really think this is the best time to start another complicated legal procedure?" I said. "Doesn't it cost a lot of money to adopt somebody?"

"That's what I'm about to go find out." Jack deposited his plate in the sink. "But I bet it's pretty routine. In fact, I bet someone in the Legal Aid Clinic could handle it."

Next thing I knew, Jack had engaged the help of the university's Legal Aid Clinic to begin adoption procedures. A senior law student, Danny Berenberg, agreed to act as our attorney.

Danny was a little younger and a little shorter than Jack; a good-looking, dark-haired, physically fit young man. In addition to being smart, he had an outgoing personality and an engaging smile. We explained what we wanted to do, and he nodded.

"Yes, of course," he said. "Partnership rights. That's an excellent reason for adoption."

Danny got right to work, with Jack helping. One day, Danny mentioned change of name, which is a common part of many adoption proceedings since it makes it clear that the adoptee is part of a family.

"I don't suppose you're planning to change either of your names?" Danny asked Jack.

"Well, I hadn't thought of it," Jack said. In a flash, he realized that a different name might offer us a better chance at getting our marriage license. "But we might want to consider that."

Danny shrugged. "It's free, if you want to do it. We

just file for the name change when we submit the adoption papers."

That evening, Jack dropped the next bombshell on our table. "You know, Michael, a lot of people change their names when they're adopted."

I reached for the salt. "I like my name just fine, Jack."

"You know your sister Pat?" he said.

"Yes, Jack, I know my sister Pat. As a matter of fact, I grew up in the same house as her."

"Well, Pat is sometimes a short form of Patricia," he said. "But sometimes, it's a guy's name—Patrick."

Now I knew where he was heading. I said, "And if you changed your name to a gender-free name, like Pat . . . and if we applied for a marriage license with your new name, how would the clerk of court know whether you were a guy or a girl?"

"Exactly." Jack grinned. "Most adoptees take the last name of their new family, and they do it for obvious reasons—so they're recognized as part of the family. I don't think the judge would balk if I changed my last name to McConnell. And if I changed my first name, too, well, that's just a matter of personal taste. Lots of people don't like the name that their parents gave them."

Brilliant! Even if our Hennepin County marriage license was rejected by the court, we could apply for another license somewhere else. With Jack using a gender-free name, there'd be no reason for anyone to question whether a man and woman were involved.

So when Danny submitted the adoption papers in Hennepin County, Judge Lindsay Arthur listened to the arguments for J. Michael McConnell's adoption of Pat Lyn

McConnell. (We chose Pat and Lyn because they were both gender-free names that were already used in the Mc-Connell family.)

Judge Arthur was known as a bit of a tyrant in Minne-apolis legal circles. He insisted on putting us through some extra hoops that we suspect he invented just for our case. Since I was making Jack my heir but I already had living relatives who could inherit my property, he said that we'd have to get my family to sign off on the adoption pro-cedure. This was time-consuming, as we needed to send official documents to Oklahoma and explain to my parents and brother and sisters what we were doing.

My family was nervous, at first, about signing their names to legal documents. They had questions about pos-sible ramifications for them, and I discussed these concerns with each of them. It actually turned out to be a positive experience for us. My parents and siblings expressed their honest feelings, and I think our exchanges strengthened the already close bonds between us. Eventually, everyone agreed to sign except my brother Jerry. I knew he had his reasons, and he never explained them to me, but he has always been a loving and supportive brother, so I didn't want to pester him about this. In spite of the missing sig-nature, Judge Arthur signed off on our adoption papers on August 3, 1971. Jack and I were delighted when we heard the news—at last, we could see an unobstructed, if uncon-ventional, path to the altar.

Timing was now critical. The Minnesota Supreme Court would likely rule on the legality of our Hennepin County license application within the next few months. After that ruling came in, the door might slam shut. If the court explicitly declared that a marriage license between two men could not be issued in Minnesota, we wouldn't be able to get a valid license anywhere in the state. We had to seize the moment.

The next day, Jack and I moved in with some friends who were living in Mankato, Minnesota, an hour-and-a-half drive southwest of the Twin Cities and located in Blue Earth County. Marilyn Montgomery was a librarian at Mankato State College. I'd known her for years, and we had worked together at Park College in Kansas City. She and her partner, Paul, lived in an apartment with their pet cats. They had an extra bedroom, and they wanted to help. Since the state marriage statutes required a couple to apply for a license in the bride's county of residence, we had our mail forwarded and lived with Marilyn and Paul for several days. Then, on August 9, I went to the Blue Earth County Courthouse and applied for a marriage license for Michael McConnell and his intended, Pat Lyn McConnell, who were residing at 107 Parkway Avenue in Mankato.

The clerk was just as friendly as she could be. We even joked about how my fiancé and I had the same last name. After I filled in our names on the form, I said, "This will be easy because there won't be any name changes involved with the same last names."

She said, "Oh yes, that's right. One of my girlfriends just married a guy with the same last name—Roberts."

Only our closest friends and family knew about our brief residence in Blue Earth County. As soon as we got back to Minneapolis, we started finalizing plans for our wedding ceremony. Everything depended, now, on timing. As soon as Mankato issued our marriage license, we needed to have everything in place for the ceremony. That way, whatever the state supreme court ruled about our Hennepin County license would not interfere with the legality of our wedding.

But secrecy isn't easy to achieve after months in the public eye. On August 16, Mankato's small newspaper, the *Free Press,* routinely printed the week's public announcements, including the notice of a marriage between James M. McConnell of Norman, Oklahoma, and Pat Lynn *[sic]* McConnell. By chance, Judy Vick, who worked for the U of M news service, noticed the announcement in her hometown paper and recognized my name. She leaked the information to reporters, and the *Minneapolis Tribune* and the *St. Paul Pioneer Press* splashed the news across their pages: that gay couple had gotten a marriage license at last!

Reporters began to call. After one conversation, Jack scowled. "That reporter just said he's seen a copy of our adoption proceedings," he said.

"So? The adoption was perfectly legal. We don't have anything to hide."

"Adoption records are confidential," Jack said. "The courthouse had no business sharing our file with reporters." He shook his head.

I shrugged. Seemed like it was always the same story: The rules were the rules—that's what we were told over and over. Except the rules never seemed to apply to people in power.

The happy couple on September 3, 1971. Photograph by Paul Hagen.

13

Groom and Groom

· · · · · · · · · · · ·

We scrambled to get all the essentials in place. Finally
we set the date: our marriage would take place on Friday
night, September 3, 1971, at 9:15 p.m.

We asked Jim Clayton, a friend who worked with
me at Gay House, to conduct our ceremony. At first Jim
agreed, but he backed out shortly before the appointed
day. He said his credentials had expired; he would attend
the ceremony to offer his well wishes and a prayer, but
he could not officiate. This left us in a real bind, but before I could panic another Gay House staff consultant, a
Methodist minister named Roger Lynn, kindly offered his
services. We didn't know him as well as Jim, but he was
clearly a liberal thinker and committed to helping the gay
community. One of his childhood friends had killed himself after being persecuted for being gay, and Roger had
never forgotten that boy's misery. At seminary, Roger's
best friend was also a gay man.

Paul Hagen, the photographer who had created Jack's
campaign posters, offered to let us use his apartment as our
venue. We had never been to Paul's place, but he told us

that he shared a tiny one-bedroom space, the top floor of a duplex, with his lover, Chris Skoglund. It was in an old home in South Minneapolis, built in the 1890s, near Chicago Avenue and Lake Street.

Paul volunteered to take care of the food. Since there wasn't time for anything elaborate, he ordered a tray of cold cuts from Bernie's Delicatessen and arranged for a three-tiered, white-frosted wedding cake. The crowning touch was a hilarious plastic groom and groom that Paul made by cutting apart two tacky wedding cake toppers and gluing the grooms together.

Terry Vanderplas, an old friend living in College Station, Texas (I had actually dated him before I met Jack), was an artist who made exquisite, original rings in silver and gold. As soon as Jack and I applied for our marriage license in Hennepin County, we asked Terry if he would be willing to create unique gold bands for our nuptials. He worked out an unusual design that looks like freeform piercings of the wide gold band. When our rings are held side by side, the openings form artful letters that spell "Mike loves Jack." Held in the other orientation, they spell "Jack loves Mike." Terry had already finished casting the eighteen-karat heavy-gauge gold bands. We called him after we got back from Mankato to say that our wedding plans had accelerated, and he promised to get the rings buffed and sent in time.

Another old friend, Charlie Walker, was a professor in the design department at Kent State University in Ohio. He created our simple wedding invitations. Using two Mars symbols for the male (open ring with an arrow emerging from it), he printed the bold, masculine design on an earth-brown background as the cover.

Since Paul's apartment was small, we gave invitations to only a very few guests. There wasn't enough time for my family in Oklahoma or Jack's sister Judy in Chicago to make travel plans to attend. But each of us chose one out-of-town friend to be best man. Jack called his best friend from high school, Mike Nealis, who lived in Chicago. Jack had been the best man at Mike's wedding, and Mike agreed to return the favor. I asked Finis Gillespie, a friend from Kansas City. Both Mike and Finis agreed to sign our marriage certificate as witnesses.

In those hectic days before the ceremony, we collaborated with two friends, each gifted writers, John Preston and Bruce Gardner, to help compose our vows for our ceremony. We wanted the words we spoke to be meaningful and authentic. I was deeply in love with Jack and glad to pledge that we would be together until death do us part. But no way was I about to agree that I would obey him!

Jack and I have never been into aping heterosexual roles, nor did we want to mock traditional marriages by staging a wedding in drag, with a bride in a frilly white gown and a groom in black tux. Instead, we invited our neighbor Steve Van Slooten to create unique wedding suits for the occasion. Steve was a clothing designer who worked for department stores like Dayton's in Minneapolis, and he made us matching white pantsuits. The bell-bottom slacks and long pullover shirts with pointy collars and bell-shaped sleeves were in a drapey polyester fabric.

They were ever so seventies. But the fabric didn't breathe well, and given the weather was sweltering on that September evening, we opted for brown leather sandals rather than closed-toe shoes.

As our preparations fell into place, lots of friends and well-wishers offered their help. We hated to tell them that they couldn't join us for the event, but there simply wasn't room in Paul's apartment for everybody that we had worked with in FREE and student government and Gay House. Many of our friends who couldn't come in person contributed small, special touches. When we arrived at Paul's apartment, we found a roomful of sentimental tokens. Streamers festooned the ceiling, flowers and homemade goodies overflowed the tables. A crystal toothpick holder filled with hand-rolled joints was one of the more memorable offerings. Two of the staffers at Gay House— Dahl Maryland and Bruce Gardner—had made macramé headbands and sent them along to complete our outfits.

That night was as hot and humid as Minneapolis ever gets. We were sweating under our polyester pantsuits before we even stepped out of our VW Bug. Upstairs, we were greeted by a dozen or so of our friends, some in summer dresses or suits and ties, others in jeans. We shook hands with Reverend Lynn. He was a few years older than we were. A slender young man around six feet tall, his dark-blond hair fell to his shirt collar. He had sky-blue eyes, a gentle smile, and an Abe Lincoln–style beard that fringed his chin. For our wedding, he dressed in a brown, Edwardian double-breasted jacket, bell-bottom slacks, and black boots. He must have been every bit as sweaty as we were.

Paul had his ancient air-conditioning unit pumping full blast, and the place was starting to feel reasonably comfortable. But a professor in speech and communications at the U of M was going to film our ceremony for a student project. When he set up his equipment and turned on his high-intensity lights, the electrical capacity of the apartment surpassed its limit. Paul hurried to the circuit box to restore the power. The filming resumed—long cords snaking across the rugs and curling beneath the guests' feet—and off went the power again. We finally realized that we could either cool the apartment or film the wedding, but not both. So we alternated between filming and cooling. When the room temperature become unbearable, we turned off the lights and camera and switched on the air conditioner.

Our actual ceremony lasted seven minutes. Reverend Lynn had brought his own Bible, and as he performed the marriage ritual, he substituted the word "spouse" for "bride" and "groom." He blended our personal words of commitment into the service. The dozen guests clapped as we ended with the traditional kiss. For some of the straight folks in the room—like our adoption attorney, Danny, and his date—that was probably the first gay kiss that they'd ever seen. But nobody seemed uncomfortable— the joy of young lovers uniting in a wedding is universal. As soon as the ceremony was finished, we turned off the air conditioner and repeated the whole thing for the film.

Before he left, Reverend Lynn placed our marriage certificate on the table. Jack and I signed it, followed by our best men. As soon as the minister signed the document, the legal requirements for our marriage were complete. Our guests applauded, aware that they had just witnessed history being made. We toasted with champagne and smiled as friends snapped photographs. There wasn't enough room for dancing, so we nibbled on the finger foods and chatted. The whole event lasted about three hours. We thanked Paul and his roommate for the use of their apartment, exchanged hugs with everyone, piled into our cars, and waved good-bye.

Outside, I turned to Jack. "We did it!" I was beaming.

"I promised I'd marry you, Michael," Jack said, his eyes reflecting the lights shining into our car's interior. "When I make a promise, I keep it."

I leaned over to kiss his cheek, and I caught a whiff of his aftershave mixed with his skin. In a rush, my mind flashed back to that heady night when I'd met Jack, at that barn dance in Norman. I remembered what Cruz said as he led me across the room to the man I would marry: "You two are destined for each other." The words had seemed silly to me at the time. But not anymore—Jack and I really were meant for each other. And that night, we fulfilled our destiny.

Back at our apartment, we opened the box that Mother had sent us. It was her wedding present—two matching knee-length robes that she sewed herself. Each was burnt orange and trimmed with colorful orange, yellow, and green braid. We stripped off our polyester wedding outfits and slipped into the soft, warm robes even though it promised to be a steamy night in Minneapolis. (And believe me, we savored every second of that steamy night!)

Near our Minneapolis apartment, early fall 1972.

14

The Highest Court in the Land

· · · · · · · · · · · · ·

I wish I could say that our wedding ceremony transformed the world overnight. That an army of lovers rose up and marched hand in hand. That all the world's people pledged to be fair to gays and straights, blacks and whites, men and women. I'm such a romantic that for a few glorious hours after our ceremony, I almost believed such a dream would come true.

Then came the reactions: Newspaper articles packed with hateful quotes. Nasty letters to the editor. Threats.

Reverend Lynn was the target of much of the venom. He was stationed at the Loring-Nicollet Center by the Minneapolis Model Cities Program, and his job was actually put in jeopardy because he'd performed our ceremony. The bishop of the United Methodist Church, Paul Washburn, claimed that Roger had performed our ceremony illegally because our license was "invalid." After that, the director of the Loring-Nicollet Center, Rev. T. Harrison Bryant, moved to cancel Roger's contract.

I was horrified. John Preston helped me organize a phone campaign. With the help of the folks at Gay House, we called around fifty agencies affiliated with the Model Cities Program. Within twenty-four hours, Bishop Washburn received so many protests that he reversed his stand. In fact, four days later, Washburn completely denied making his comments about Roger.

Jack and I were immensely relieved that Roger didn't lose his job because he'd had the courage to marry us. But we weren't sure if our marriage was safe from other attempts at retaliation. Would the officials in Blue Earth County attempt legal action against us?

When the word had first leaked about our Mankato license, the Blue Earth County attorney had gone on record claiming our license was "defective." Since there was no bride, he said we didn't fulfill the requirement that a bride has to reside in the county where a marriage license was issued. And although none of the statutes specified how long a bride must live in a county before claiming residence, the county attorney complained that we weren't listed as either renters or owners of Marilyn and Paul's apartment, so how could we claim residence? Reporters attempted to contact Marilyn and Paul to question them about our residency, but our friends refused to take the calls.

By this point in our lives, we had learned to be wary of the powers that be. Officials had demonstrated to us that they were willing to ignore their own laws in order to suppress our right to love. We sent our marriage certificate to Blue Earth County by certified mail, properly signed, and we kept the post office's confirmation that it arrived. When reporters contacted the Blue Earth County attorney, he said it would not be filed. However, nobody from Blue Earth County ever contested our marriage in court, and since we had fulfilled all the legal requirements, it meant that our wedding vows remained sanctified by the law.

As I had learned in my dealings with the university's Board of Regents, officials are often stubborn people. Blue Earth County is still—over four decades later—unwilling to recognize the license it issued and affirm that our marriage took place. In 2014, as I was preparing our files for donation to the Tretter Collection (the archive of GLBT materials at the U of M), I contacted Blue Earth County again. I requested a certified copy of our marriage record so I could include it with our other documents. To my astonishment, I received this opaque reply: "Our office is unable to locate a record as stated in your request." I hired an attorney to investigate, and he obtained from the county clerk in Vitals a copy of all our records in their files. As we expected, the Blue Earth County files clearly show that the proper office received our marriage certificate in September 1971, but it had never been recorded. An unsigned letter was also in our file. It was on letterhead stationery from the county attorney's office, and it said that our marriage certificate "need not be recorded." It gave no justification for what was described as "my opinion." My attorney wrote to the county and patiently explained that our license was lawfully issued and that "no court ordered Marriage Record No. 22 to be annulled, then or ever." He also warned the officials that continued refusal to record it would be seen as a deliberate denial of a constitutional right to enjoy equal protection under law. The assistant county attorney, Mark A. Lindahl, responded in February 2015: the county will not "provide you with certified copies of the marriage record."

Can you believe it? Nearly a half century later, Blue Earth County is still refusing to comply with its legal obligation! Of course, in the end, it doesn't matter how stubborn these petty officials are. As far as I'm concerned, they can take their sullen pouts with them all the way to the grave because the law of contracts is clear: a validated document remains legal even if a functionary refuses to recognize it. Only a court can decide otherwise.

Even though we had been legally married using our Mankato license, our court battles weren't over in 1971. The Minnesota Supreme Court ruling was still pending on *Baker v. Nelson,* our earlier request for a license from Hennepin County. On October 15, 1971, about six weeks after our wedding was solemnized, the court finally returned its decision. It came as no surprise that the justices unanimously rejected our appeal. But I found the wording of the ruling incredible. In this country, built on the principle of separation of church and state, the court actually cited the Book of Genesis to deny our lawful rights. The judges stated that marriage involved "the procreation and rearing of children within a family." In answer to the obvious objection that heterosexual couples are not required to procreate, the ruling stated that " 'abstract symmetry' is not demanded by the Fourteenth Amendment."

"Sounds like a review of an art exhibit," I said. "What does 'abstract symmetry' have to do with constitutional rights?"

"The judges are trying to justify discrimination," Jack explained. "They're saying it's okay for heterosexuals to marry without any intention of having kids, but since gay men can't procreate, they can't marry. What applies to one group doesn't have to apply to the other. The law doesn't have to be symmetrical."

"Well, that's fair," I growled. "Let's just have equal rights for everybody . . . except for the people we don't happen to agree with."

We talked about what we should do next. Since we had already found another way to marry, we could have just dropped the Hennepin County lawsuit at that point. But Jack was for pressing on.

"The next step is the U.S. Supreme Court," he said. "We've gone this far; I say we keep going. If the U.S. Supreme Court reviews our case, they'll have to issue a ruling on gay marriage. It's worth the try."

Continuing the lawsuit would be a drain on us, but I knew that Jack was right. We had found a loophole for ourselves and managed to get married, but the gate was still locked for other gay couples. If we kept this lawsuit going and the U.S. Supreme Court ruled that our marriage application must be accepted, then marriage would become legal for every gay couple in America. It had been months since the *Look* feature was published, but letters kept coming from gay teens who saw us as role models, as torchbearers. In my work at Gay House, I had seen the terrible effects of discrimination on fine young people who happened to be gay. This battle wasn't just about us.

I nodded. "Okay. Let's go for it."

Three days later we heard the ruling in our other big lawsuit—*McConnell v. Andersen*—my job discrimination case. It was a bitter disappointment. The Eighth U.S.

Circuit Court of Appeals in St. Louis reversed Judge Neville's decision, and the injunction against the university was lifted. That meant the Regents' rejection of my job offer would stand. Putting it in the language of the schoolyard: a big bully known as the University of Minnesota was going to get away with stomping on my civil rights.

"This is bullshit!" I fumed as I read the ruling. "All the damn circuit court did was live up to its name by inventing circuitous arguments. The judges didn't even look at the university's hiring practices. How could they rule on a civil rights case without looking at whether my employer violated my civil rights? It makes no sense."

I was trembling all over and on the brink of tears. After all these months, after all the hours we'd poured into researching, after all the days going over the case with my lawyers, my lawsuit had been struck down. And for the flimsiest of reasons. Jack put his arms around me and held me close.

He made me some herbal tea, and when I calmed down, we read through the ruling together. The judges had focused on my "activist role" in promoting what they described as a "socially repugnant concept." They were implying that it was my fault for losing my job because I didn't pursue my "homosexual propensities" in a "clandestine" manner.

"Good grief!" I said. "These judges want me to be 'clandestine.' Can you imagine?" I felt like I'd fallen down Alice's rabbit hole into some sort of bizarre wonderland. Apparently the judges thought that I deserved to lose my job because I hadn't kept my mouth shut. Since when do courts rule against someone for being honest?

The judges said that I'd tried to "foist tacit approval . . . on an institution of higher learning" by my behavior. Yes, they wrote the word "foist" as if I were the aggressor! Were they kidding? The University of Minnesota was a big powerful institution run with public monies. I was just one young man expecting fair treatment according to our nation's laws. Since when do courts need to protect Goliath against little David?

"It seems incredible," Jack said. He massaged my neck and shoulders. "Instead of reprimanding the university for wrongdoing, the court blamed the victim."

We weren't the only ones who felt outraged by the circuit court's ruling. The *Minneapolis Star* editorialized about it. Eugene McCarthy, a senator and a presidential contender at the time, called the court's reasoning "nonsense." The Minnesota Civil Liberties Union, the NAACP, Minneapolis Urban Coalition, and others endorsed a campus rally to support me. At the rally, hundreds of students, faculty, and staff members gathered in front of Morrill Hall. I appreciated their support, and I tried hard to put on a brave face at the rally.

Although I didn't realize it at the time, one of the people who attended that campus demonstration was Allan Spear, then an associate professor of history at the U of M. Spear went on to become president of the Minnesota Senate and one of the first openly gay state legislators in the country. When he attended the rally, Spear was still in the closet. In his autobiography, *Crossing the Barriers,* which was published two years after his death, Spear wrote that this was the very first gay rights demonstration that he ever attended. It was a life-changing experience for him. He said, "I finally was beginning to see gay rights as a basic civil rights issue; this was job discrimination pure and simple and was no more permissible than racial discrimination."

Jack and I got to know Spear, and over the years we maintained a somewhat rocky relationship with him as we participated in DFL political events. We always considered him a hesitant standard-bearer—at best—for gay rights. A closeted man for much of his career, he acknowledged being gay only after quite a bit of public pressure. (Apparently we also had something to do with his coming out: he wrote that it was our "courageous work" with FREE that "would force me to come to terms with my sexuality.")

Of course I had no way of knowing that this rally would influence Allan Spear—or anyone else—to demand an end to job discrimination against gays. Looking back, I find such thoughts consoling. But during the rally, I had all I could do to stand tall and speak to the crowd. A sick feeling in the pit of my stomach kept reminding me that all of these other people would go back to their classes and their careers, and I would still be the man without a job. I would still be the man facing an uncertain future. I didn't know if I would ever be able to do the work that I had trained for. I didn't know if I had thrown away thousands of dollars and as many hours preparing for a library position that I would never hold. It was fine and good for all these people to show their solidarity and sympathy for me. But would any library ever have the courage to hire me?

Deep down, and in spite of these painful doubts, I was and am an optimist. I kept hoping that scholars would eventually force justice to prevail, that fellow librarians would somehow force the Board of Regents to reconsider. I had submitted my request for action paper to the American Library Association's Intellectual Freedom Committee that January. Unfortunately, a professor in the University of Minnesota's Library School named David Berninghausen chaired that committee. The committee decided not to act, citing the flimsy reason that my request "did not discuss how the infringement . . . violated the spirit of the Library Bill of Rights."

Another example of double-talk! Berninghausen's committee was twiddling thumbs and shuffling papers while ignoring flagrant discrimination. Incensed, I decided to go to the annual ALA conference, to be held that June in Dallas, Texas, to try and win support among my library colleagues.

Although I forced myself to keep talking brave and appearing confident, these public confrontations were becoming more and more difficult for me. Before each court hearing or demonstration, I would have anxiety attacks. I had trouble sleeping. During the day, my worries gnawed at me.

Jack knew how painful my job crusade was. He offered to go with me to Texas. Other librarians active in the ALA Task Force on Gay Liberation also showed up and demonstrated their solidarity, among them Israel Fishman and Steve Wolf, as well as Barbara Gittings and Kay Tobin (the lesbian couple who had worked with Frank Kameney and other early leaders to promote gay rights). We staged a heated confrontation in a hall filled with seven hundred librarians. This finally forced the Intellectual Freedom Committee to take some kind of action. But all the members managed to produce were two tepid resolutions: "Based on the decision of the Federal District Court of Minnesota, J. Michael McConnell's rights . . . have been violated," and that my case should be given high priority in yet another ALA committee, the Committee on Mediation, Arbitration, and Inquiry. It wasn't much, but at least the committee acknowledged that the university had discriminated against me. Unfortunately, all they were going to do about it was instruct one of their committees to notify another. What good would that do?

Although I continued to pursue redress through my professional organization for the next four years at various meetings and conferences, the ALA never took meaningful action. They refused to issue a formal statement objecting to the way the university had treated me. Maybe I harbored a Pollyana-ish view, but I had always revered librarians as the sacred keepers of knowledge, the priests and priestesses of intellectual freedom. I couldn't help feeling resentful. How could my colleagues ignore this opportunity to translate ideals into real life?

Meanwhile, the MCLU had requested a rehearing of my case, but this was denied by the full court of appeals. At this point, I had no choice but to go before the highest court in the land. With the ACLU backing me, I appealed to the U.S. Supreme Court. In my petition, I stated that if the circuit court's ruling was allowed to stand, "millions of Americans may be unconstitutionally barred from employment simply because they are homosexuals."

So in the landmark year of our marriage, Jack and I found ourselves in the extraordinary situation of bringing two cases before the U.S. Supreme Court.

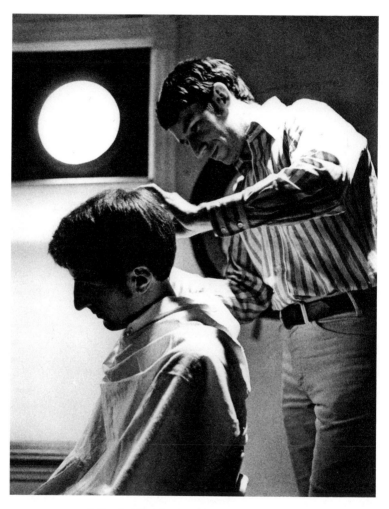

Cutting Jack's hair for the Look *magazine feature, 1970.*
Photograph by Charlotte Brooks.

15

Married Life

· · · · · · · · · · · · · ·

In the fall of 1971 we were at last beginning our life together as a lawfully wedded couple. I wouldn't term this our honeymoon period, though. Our daily lives hardly changed at all after our wedding. We still shared an apartment with Mike Wetherbee and Jim DeVillier. Our classes and projects still ate up all of our time. Jack was immersed in his third-year law classes as well as busy with the demands on a student body president. As for me, entering my second year of underemployment, I was determined to make my days valuable. I devoted every spare hour to my pet project: organizing and providing social services for the off-campus gay community through Gay House. At night, I scraped together whatever earnings I could as a bartender. Both of our lawsuits (*Baker v. Nelson,* concerning our Hennepin County marriage license, and *McConnell v. Andersen,* the University of Minnesota's denial of my employment) continued to wind through the courts.

We were paying for Jack's law school with his veteran's benefits, and he was entitled to an increase in those benefits since he now had a family with dependents. We really needed the additional money, so he decided to apply. But our family situation was a bit unusual since I was both Jack's adopted father and his lawful spouse. Should he apply for benefits for me as his parent or as his spouse?

Jack decided to try to get increased benefits for me as his "dependent parent" first, and he submitted an application in September. The Veterans Administration promptly rejected it on the grounds that that our child–parent relationship had begun after Jack had already turned twenty-one. He appealed, and the VA board rejected his application again, this time because my income (paltry as it was) exceeded my expenses.

We did manage to bring in a little money from our public speaking. Jack's activism had made him a sought-after lecturer. I often accompanied him and shared the stage when we addressed groups of teachers, church groups, and campus gatherings. We usually received some kind of honorarium, although the money was barely enough to cover our gas if we had to drive to the far reaches of the state. But we knew that we had become objects of curiosity by living, loving, and marrying in the open. People are scared of the unknown. By meeting folks in small towns away from the glare of the spotlight, by answering questions honestly and politely, we could make a real difference in attitudes. Our hope was that these small changes would eventually produce a big difference in the way gay men and women were treated.

We were invited to discuss gay issues outside the state as well. In December 1971, we spoke at the State University of New York in Albany. A month later, Jack shared a podium with lesbian activist Barbara Gittings at the

University of Alabama in Huntsville. Just two weeks after that, we crossed the border to speak at Canada's York University outside Toronto. Over two thousand gathered at the University of Manitoba in Winnipeg in March to hear Jack's lecture, "The Right to Be Human and Gay." His speech generated so much interest that it was reprinted in the *Manitoban,* the campus newspaper, along with the question and answer session that followed. Jack talked in detail about our attempts to marry and the lawsuits that had resulted. Although I had heard Jack's speech many times, I never tired of watching him engage an audience as he began with this brief but eloquent statement of what we both believe:

> I think the right to be gay is the right to be human without being ridiculed. The concept that we must all be the same, that we must all dress alike, that we must all make love alike, that we must all go to the same church, to me again is another perversion of society. I think that we are different and that we must respect those differences. And that we, as individuals, as human beings, must allow for differences, and allow for differences in each individual without intimidating and without ridicule.
>
> I think the right to be gay is the right to have equal rights under the law. That's the right to job protection. Simply because we make love in a different manner does not mean that person is not entitled to a living wage, does not mean that person is not entitled to job protection under the law, does not mean that person is not entitled to housing

protection. These are rights that are guaranteed us through our humanity, regardless of what country we are born in, whether in this country or in the United States. And I think also it means the right to make love as you see fit and not as some other person sees fit. So that basically is what the right to be gay means to me. I think it's really a very simple concept. It's really, to summarize, the right to be human.

We also appeared on radio talk shows and TV news shows. *Kennedy & Co,* a talk show aired by ABC, flew us to Chicago to appear on one of their September shows. We were on *The Dave Moore Show* several times; a portion of our wedding tape was aired on one of Moore's shows. In 1973, we were flown to New York to appear on the influential *David Susskind Show.* We also made several appearances on *The Phil Donahue Show.* As a result of these appearances, we received mail from viewers around the country.

Meanwhile, on the University of Minnesota campus, Jack's leadership was making visible inroads. A student now sat as a nonvoting member of every Regents' committee. His student government had formed a corporation, opened a campus store, and established a student housing bureau. As fall turned to winter, we could see that these ambitious projects would require more than just a one-year term in office if they were going to have a lasting impact. Jack had missed a deadline for enrolling in one of the required courses in the law school sequence, so he knew that he'd need to remain at the university for an extra term to complete his coursework. (Luckily, his veteran's benefits would extend into a fourth year.) Since he would be on campus for another year, he decided to run for reelection.

If Jack won a second term, he would set another record: In the university's 121-year history, no student body president had ever won reelection. In March 1972, Jack entered a primary against nine other candidates. For this race, a primary had replaced the former procedure in which the MSA Forum selected three candidates to run in the campus-wide election. Jack's campaign strategy emphasized his accomplishments as president, and he received 43 percent of roughly 4,400 votes cast in the primary. He faced two opponents in the general election and won handily, with over 3,000 of 7,400 votes cast.

I was pleased by the students' vote of confidence in my husband, but April 1972 was not a happy month for me. I received the final decision in the lawsuit for my university job, *McConnell v. Andersen*. Rather than a triumph, or even a thoughtful review of my case, I got a fizzle. Since my case involved job discrimination, the U.S. Supreme Court could choose whether or not to review it. The court chose not to. (Only one of the justices, William O. Douglas, indicated that he was willing to hear my case.)

After two years and all those briefs, court appearances, and appeals, I'd run up against a dead end.

I was disappointed and exhausted. In the two years that it had taken for my case to snake through the courts, I'd begun to think of it as the dark monster that fed on my inner peace. Yes, I put on a cheerful face every day as I worked with troubled young people at Gay House. But

I was worn out by the constant anxiety about my future. When I finally got word about the lawsuit's outcome, I was more than ready for it to be over, even though I knew the court's decision was terribly wrong.

Jack's reaction was different from mine. He was angry. He demanded that the university reveal how much money it had spent *not* to hire me, and the answer was stunning: $25,000. That was more than twice what it would have cost them to pay my salary during the two years that the case had dragged on. In other words, they could have gotten ten two full years of work from a competent librarian for less than it cost them to discriminate against me. Not to mention what it did to their public image.

While my suit was pending, I had refrained from applying for other library positions because I didn't want to prejudice my case. That forced me to spend two long years working outside my chosen field. As far as I was concerned, the best thing about the U.S. Supreme Court ruling was that I could finally return to the work that I love.

I immediately set out hunting for a library job. I didn't want to move away from Jack, of course, so I concentrated on libraries located in or near the Twin Cities. I knew the job market in my field was tight, and I feared that all the publicity over our marriage and my lawsuit had made me a pariah in our area. I figured that it would take a lot of guts to hire someone who had received the kind of notoriety that I had. But I was determined to get back into library work, so I was prepared to take anything, even if it meant starting all over on the bottom rung.

As the months passed, I submitted job applications to an ever-widening ring of libraries. Finally, I saw a part-time opening for a clerk posted by the Hennepin County Library system. They were looking for somebody in technical services, which is one of my areas of expertise. The position was a big step down for me—I had been a senior-level librarian in an academic library at Park College, and this was merely an entry-level job in a public library system. Not only that, the salary was so low that I would need to keep bartending at night. But it was a library job, so I applied and was pleased when they offered me the job. I started in 1973, and the following year, I moved into a full-time position.

Meanwhile, we were still awaiting the U.S. Supreme Court decision on *Baker v. Nelson,* concerning our Hennepin County marriage license. In this case, Jack had asked Minnesota's Supreme Court to recognize an inherent right of same-sex couples to marry. The way he posed the legal question was critical—he purposefully framed the legal question so that it involved a state's interpretation of the federal constitution. He knew the U.S. Supreme Court was required to review any case that came before it involving this kind of question. Furthermore, this kind of case would be allowed to bypass the lower courts and be appealed directly to the U.S. Supreme Court. (Congress has since abolished this option.) Lawyers for Hennepin County insisted that there was no need for the high court to decide our claim because all issues had been resolved when Blue Earth County issued us a marriage license.

In the fall of 1972, Jack entered his last term of law school with plans for a December graduation. That October, we finally received the U.S. Supreme Court's reply: another fizzle. The judges dismissed our case "for want of a substantial federal question." That's courtspeak. Jack said it meant that the court was not ready to answer the question that our case posed at that time. In other words, the court did not reject our claim; instead, it chose not to hear our case, so Minnesota's decision would be allowed to stand. Since marriage contracts are traditionally governed by the states, the U.S. Supreme Court would step into this area only if it saw a blatant inequality in a state's action.

But the meaning of the words "for want of a substantial federal question" was fuzzy enough to cause a debate among legal scholars that lasted for over four decades. In a column carried by the *New York Times* ("Wedding Bells," in the Opinionator, March 20, 2013), Linda Greenhouse wrote that the court's action was "a formulaic way" to say "there is so little to this case that we don't even have to bother hearing it." She also wrote that our case has been cited as a precedent for courts hearing gay marriage cases ever since. (Perhaps that explains why the U.S. Supreme Court felt the need to declare "*Baker v. Nelson* must be and is now overruled" when it finally ruled on gay marriage in 2015.)

Looking back on what I call this "landmark indecision," it seems like a crying shame. The highest court in our country walked away from a priceless opportunity to champion human rights. So many hours of effort, so many dollars spent, and so many tears have been shed in the intervening years to establish marriage equality. All of that might have been spared if only the court had showed more courage in 1972.

I can't say that either of us was surprised by the ruling,

though. We've always dreamed big, Jack and I. But we've always been realists, too.

"We'll just keep hammering away," Jack said. "That's all we can do. Keep it in the public eye. In the newspaper headlines."

"What do you mean?" I said. "I thought the Supreme Court was the end of the road. We've gone as far as we can go."

"The Supreme Court is the highway, but there are other ways to get where we want to go. We'll take the back roads—like applying to the VA for spousal bene-fits. The IRS is another arm of government. They'll have to rule on our marriage when we apply for a joint tax return."

I groaned. "All that will take years."

He shrugged. "Hey, we're going to spend the rest of our life together. Right?"

"But lawsuits take time, Jack. Money. What about the rest of our dreams? A home? Career? Kids?"

He looked at me. "I can promise you a home, Mi-chael—a home you'll be proud of. And you're good at your work, so I know you'll have your career." He raised his eyebrows and let out a long breath. "But I didn't know kids were part of the bargain. Can you settle for an 'I'll do my best' on that one?"

I've never been good at settling for less than a full serv-ing, but I kissed his cheek and said, "I guess I can wait a while to have it all. First we'll get you through law school and past the bar exam, and then we'll move into our next chapter."

In the midst of remodeling our new home, September 1980.

16

Back Roads

. . . .

Jack finished his law school classes in December 1972. After the first of the year in 1973, the university informed him that he would not be permitted to continue as student body president since he was no longer registered as a student. Jack protested, of course. But by the time the case went to trial, his term in office had run out.

That was annoying, but he was already embroiled in other controversies. The previous November, he applied to take the bar exam and was immediately opposed by a local Baptist minister named Rev. Joseph Head, who was president of the area chapter of the Sons of the American Revolution as well as an organization called Citizens for Preservation of the University of Minnesota. In November 1972, Head sent a letter to the editor at the *Minnesota Daily* accusing Jack of "socialism, subversion, and homosexuality." As a result, the director of bar admissions summoned Jack to a meeting to examine his moral qualifications. Specifically, the committee delved into a charge of fraud based on our application for a marriage license in Blue Earth County.

In December, the committee ruled that Jack would be permitted to take the bar. He didn't pass on his first try, so he reapplied. Meanwhile he made a bid to enter local politics: he campaigned for the second ward alderman seat on the Minneapolis City Council. Jack's campaign did not focus on his well-known reputation as a gay candidate. Instead, his platform addressed green issues—bike paths, rapid transit, zoning, and neighborhood concerns. Jack was unsuccessful in both his bid for the alderman seat and his second try at the bar exam.

"It's no wonder you didn't pass the bar," I said. "Between campaigning for the city council and all your public speaking, you don't have time to breathe. Maybe you better drop everything else for a few months and just concentrate on getting ready for the exam?"

"I'm not sure that my scores have anything to do with how much I study," Jack said. "Or with the answers that I gave to the questions."

"What do you mean?"

"I really don't think the bar association wants me to have a license to practice law."

"Can you request copies of your tests to see how they were scored?" I said.

"No, all test information is sealed. There's no way to prove that there was any behind-the-scenes tampering with the scores."

In spite of his suspicions, Jack retook the bar exam in February 1974. This time, he did pass, and that summer he began his practice. He opened an office in Loring Park with our apartment-mate, Mike Wetherbee. Loring Park was considered the "gay ghetto" of Minneapolis, but Jack and Wetherbee didn't plan to limit their practice to gay issues. They took a variety of cases—divorces, wills, misdemeanors, business issues, and other general practice items.

Meanwhile, we kept "traveling the back roads," as Jack put it, to have our marriage recognized by the government. In April, we initiated a case against the IRS because they had rejected our last two tax forms, which we'd filed jointly as a married couple. (By filing jointly, we actually paid more taxes than if we had filed as single individuals, so the IRS sent us a refund check. To prove our point, we refused to cash it.) Jack appealed to the VA for the educational benefits that had not been granted to him—as a married veteran attending law school, he should have been entitled to them. Both of these cases began snaking through courts and review boards while we continued our activities in local politics. Jack worked with a member of the council to draft an amendment to the city's human rights bill that prohibited discrimination on the basis of "affectional or sexual preference." This amendment passed, making Minneapolis one of the nation's first cities to outlaw discrimination against gays in housing, employment, and public accommodations.

At this point, Jack and I were in our early thirties, our education was complete, and both of us had decent jobs. We were married, in a stable and loving relationship. The biological clock was ticking, and we began soul-searching: did we want to bring a child into our lives? If so, it was time to start the process. We both felt that if we delayed much longer, we would be past the prime years for being a parent. If we were going to raise a child, we wanted to do it while we had the energy of our youth. We also felt it was better for the child to have fairly young parents who were attuned to the changing culture.

Adopting a child was not a casual decision for us. We had been discussing it for years, and we knew it would be a gigantic change to go from a household of two young professionals to a family that included a child. I grew up in a big family nurtured by wonderful parents, and my siblings all had families, so I had plenty of role models for parenting. Although Jack was orphaned at a young age and raised in a boarding school, I had seen him around our friends' children. He was attentive, kind, patient, and nurturing. I knew he would make a fine dad.

Our friends often urged us to consider adopting a child when they watched us playing with their kids or with our pets. Over the years, a succession of cats—Lotus, Socko, Tyler, and Tabatha—graced our home. Their gleaming coats and affectionate mannerisms were proof that we doted on them. Through our public speaking, we had interacted with many high school students. We were proud that we had been strong, inspiring role models for them, and we felt that working with those teens had enriched our lives.

With the possibility of adopting our own child in mind, we began keeping track of cases in the news involving gay couples as parents. By the end of 1973, both the American Psychiatric and Psychological Associations removed "homosexuality" from their lists of mental disorders, and professionals no longer contended that being gay was a sickness. But since gay lovers were prohibited from marrying, children could only be adopted by one individual in the relationship. This put gay couples seeking adoption at a terrible disadvantage. They would always be placed low on the list of prospective parents because they were considered single parents by adoption agencies.

Realistically, we stood a very slim chance of adopting a healthy, American-born Caucasian baby because there were long waiting lists for these children. But this wasn't a stumbling block for us. We had already talked over the possibility of adopting an older child, as well as a child of a different race, or a child who had health concerns. We decided that we were willing to adopt any child under the age of six. We knew we could be loving parents for a child of any ethnic background, and we had plenty of fine, strong female friends who would be role models if we adopted a girl. We were also willing to adopt a child with health concerns, as long as our income was sufficient to provide for whatever the child needed.

After thinking long and hard, we decided that yes, we could offer a child a wonderful home. And bringing a child into our lives would give us pleasure and joy. So we began the adoption process. At first, we tried the standard route and submitted applications to three adoption agencies in the Twin Cities. Two of them informed us that very few children were available but they would keep our application on file. We assured them that we were willing to wait. The third agency, the Children's Home Society of Minnesota, told us that they didn't consider us appropriate parents. Since this group accepted funding from United Way, Jack filed a complaint with that agency as well as with the St. Paul Department of Civil Rights.

We attended preadoption meetings at the agencies and talked with couples who had successfully adopted. We even tossed around ideas about how we should alter our home to suit the needs of a child. Jack investigated how we could add a child to our health care policy. Both of us are attentive to details; Jack's background in the law and engineering predisposes him to precise detail work, and of course my library background shows that I am detail oriented. We felt that parenthood was a big responsibility, and if we were going to do it well, we needed to immerse ourselves in learning, planning, and arranging.

Every few months, one of us called to check on our application with the adoption agencies. This went on for two years. We realized at the start that it was going to take quite a while—at best—before we would be able to adopt through the standard route. But it was starting to seem hopeless, like we were heaving our fondest desires into a dark pit. I found myself staring at the wall after Jack reported that yet another phone call had produced yet another disappointing response. After these calls, we'd chew our supper in silence, each of us absorbed in his own empty musings.

Around this time, one of our friends discovered that she was pregnant. She had some personal difficulties that would make child rearing awkward if not impossible. So she approached us about the possibility of having us adopt her baby. We were delighted, but we thought it would be best to wait and give her time to reconsider before making any formal arrangements. This seemed like our best shot at bringing a child into our lives. We tried not to get too excited about the prospect, knowing that she might find a way to work through her problems and keep her child. But it was hard to put a lid on our enthusiasm. We chatted

about how to decorate the nursery, and we started looking at baby furniture. We found ourselves grinning about
what fun it was going to be to share our dinnertime with a
chubby baby in a high chair. When our friend eventually
decided that she would keep her child, we told her that we
understood and wanted the best for her. But the truth was,
we were awfully disheartened.

Eventually, we let our applications at the adoption
agencies lapse. It just seemed less and less likely that we
would ever be able to adopt a child. It felt like we were
reopening a wound every time we contacted the adoption
agencies and heard another "no, not yet." Rather than
dwell on the impossible, we decided to focus on things
that we could accomplish instead.

In the mid-1970s, Jack stumbled on a shocking conflict
of interest involving Minnesota's public officials and jour-
nalists. Minnesota was one of the first places in the United
States to have a news council, which is an independent
panel created to examine complaints about news report-
ing. These complaints might involve challenges to the ac-
curacy of news reports or accusations of bias on the part of
reporters. Obviously, public officials often have a vested
interest in the outcome of these cases, so news councils
are supposed to operate independently of all official influence. But Jack discovered that the corporate office of the
Minnesota News Council and the offices of the Minnesota
Supreme Court shared the same address. In other words,
the news council was operating from the chambers of the
court! Some further investigation led Jack to an even more
shocking discovery: one of the supreme court justices
served as the head of the news council. Jack was sure this

entire arrangement was unethical, if not downright illegal. He decided that the best way to correct the situation was by exposing it to the public. So he ran for a seat on the supreme court against the justice who headed the news council. He lost the election, but he made a second run in the 1980 election. In all, Jack ran in five state supreme court elections between 1978 and 2002. Shortly thereafter, the news council finally dissociated itself from the court. I will always believe that Jack's persistence was the reason for this long-overdue separation of court and council.

By 1979, we were looking for a house to buy. We found a neglected house not too far from Lake Calhoun in Minneapolis that was being used as a three-unit rental. It had fallen into such disrepair that some of its walls were literally caving in. But the building had character as well as potential: it was originally built as a farmhouse in the 1850s from trees in the forest where the city of Minneapolis now stands. In the 1920s, the building was moved to its present location and converted to Craftsman style. As soon as we purchased it, we began making plans to restore the building.

Wetherbee had moved away, and Jack decided that he would prefer to work from home so he could supervise the massive renovation of our house. Both of us consider our home the tangible symbol of our love. That's why we have spent so many years lavishing both our attention and money on this project. Soon after we bought our home, Jack and I came to a life-altering decision: it was time to step out of our activist roles.

Jack had been heavily involved with local politics and gay activism ever since he arrived in Minnesota. Frankly,

the thrill had worn off. He was tired of the demands of
public appearances, the travel and hours spent with sometimes hostile strangers. He wanted to nourish our life
together.

I had been gradually moving up the ranks of the Hennepin County Library system. By 1980, I had reached the
position of senior librarian. I had staff members and other
librarians under my supervision. My job was very meaningful to me. In a public library system, I could influence
lives by providing vital information to people who really
needed it. I was also working with new library computer
systems, as I did when I worked at the academic library at
Park College. I felt like I had the best of both worlds in
my library work: I was helping to redesign and streamline
information services. And I was making a difference in
people's lives, just as I had at Gay House.

The focus of the gay rights movement had also
changed. Once AIDS was identified, the conversation had
shifted to medical care and funding to find a cure. We
felt these issues were best handled by a new generation of
leaders. Jack and I had fought for the right to marry, and
we had found our own way to make our vision a reality.
We hoped that other gay men and women would soon
follow in our footsteps and enjoy the right to marry and
live openly, with dignity and pride. It was time for us to be
silent and let younger singers take the microphone.

It's the law! In June 2015, the Supreme Court of the United States announced that "same-sex couples may exercise the fundamental right to marry." The court's ruling included the note that Minnesota's 1972 decision in "Baker v. Nelson must be and now is overruled." Photograph by Angela Jimenez.

17

Ever After

. . . .

Nearly forty-three years to the day after Jack and I applied for our marriage license in Hennepin County, justice prevailed. Our state, Minnesota, became the twelfth state to legalize marriage for all lovers on May 13, 2013. I was there to witness the historic vote in the state senate.

Yes, it was glorious! Rainbow flags flew from the posts along St. Paul's Wabasha Bridge. Not to be outdone, the I-35 bridge in neighboring Minneapolis turned magical after dark as a rainbow of candy-colored lights lit the pedestrian walkway. Underneath, where thick pillars stand tall and proud, the bridge was bathed in a soft lavender glow.

There were two lines waiting at the door to get into the senate chambers that morning. I counted six people ahead of me in the preticketed line. All around us, people streamed through the Capitol's halls and into the rotunda. The atmosphere was festive, with lots of people wearing bright orange T-shirts emblazoned with slogans announcing their support of the bill. I saw people of all ages holding banners and signs, gay couples tenderly holding hands, excited kids with scrubbed faces hopping from foot to foot. People waved and flashed smiles as they spotted friends in the crowd. My mind flashed back to the vision that I had conjured after Jack and I were wed in 1971—at long last, my army of lovers had arisen. Announcing their joy in an explosion of orange, the soldiers of justice had taken the Capitol.

The six folks in front of me in line looked drab by comparison. They were among the small but vocal opposition; I knew that because they were complaining in loud voices about the upcoming vote. I have to admit that I smirked as I slid past those naysayers on my way into the gallery. All their protests, all their hate had amounted to nothing more than pissing in the wind. On the previous Friday, the Minnesota House had passed the marriage bill by a wide margin, and we knew we had enough votes for the bill to pass in the Senate that day.

Seated in the gallery under soft lighting, the air felt cool and fresh. But by the time the two-hour debate had finished, it was starting to warm up and my knees were beginning to stiffen. We were packed into tight rows, almost like the seats on an airplane. But the slight discomfort was a small price to pay for the elation that I felt, surrounded by friends and people that I admired. Seated near me was Ann DeGroot, former leader of OutFront Minnesota. Laurie and Gloria, a couple from the northern part of the state, introduced themselves. I grinned when they told me that they were looking forward to being married. I met a man named Bill, a professional who was seated with his lover. A young fellow from Minnetonka named Shaun shook my hand and told me that he'd helped to campaign for the soon-to-be law.

A row of reporters and TV cameras was positioned two steps down from my seat and partially blocked my view of the senate floor. I peered between the cameras to watch key speakers stand up. I'm sure that I was smiling when Scott Dibble began his remarks. Scott Dibble is the openly gay senator from Minneapolis who was the sponsor of the marriage equality bill.

As one of our state's legislative spokespeople for gay rights, he is often considered the successor to Allan Spear, the U of M history professor who retired as president of the Minnesota Senate in 2000. But everything about Dibble's demeanor reflects how the times have changed and for the better. Unlike his successor, Spear never had the courage or foresight to take a public stand in favor of marriage equality.

Scott Dibble is tall, proud, and dignified. He has been a courageous leader and spokesperson on many controversial issues. He married his lover in California in 2008 before the passage of Proposition 8, and he has championed marriage equality as well as other legislation for members of the GLBT community and minorities.

As always, he spoke with intelligence and eloquence that morning in the senate chambers. He explained that the marriage equality bill wouldn't diminish other legislation—only add to it.

Yes, I couldn't agree more! And it was clear that the crowd felt the same. I could hear the cheers from the rotunda, where the speeches were being telecast from the senate floor. Even through the thick walls and heavy,

massive doors, the sounds of the excited crowd were un-
mistakable. After the actual passage of the bill, the cheer-
ing rose to a roar. It sounded like a massive sporting event
in a crowded stadium.

In the chambers, my smile threatened to burst my
cheeks when Senator Tony Lourey stood. As far as I was
concerned, he summarized it all with three short and gorgeous words: "Today, love wins."

I wanted to hug him—to sing and shout and dance!
Tony is the son of Becky Lourey, a former state senator and candidate for governor who once lived near us
in Minneapolis and has remained friends with us for four
decades. Jack and I watched him grow into a proud, able
champion of people's rights.

Yes, it was exhilarating to be sitting there. Hundreds of
fair-minded people shared this historic moment with me—
men and women, gay and straight. We had been on the
side of justice for decades. Now, at last, we were also on
the side of victory. I am just so happy that Jack and I were
alive to see our dream become a reality for all gay men
and women in this state that has been our beloved home.

Love is the most powerful force in the universe. Jack
and I have always known this. We trusted that love would
prevail over hate and ignorance and religious intolerance.
It has.

Lots of things have changed since Jack and I stepped away
from our activist roles. Openly gay men and women are
now smiling at the world from TV screens and movie
theaters as well as the galleries of the senate. Openly gay
couples hold hands and embrace in public.

Gay Pride events attract tens of thousands of supporters
—straight as well as gay. Whole families come out to clap
for the most colorful costumes and catch wrapped candies
tossed from the floats. Children hold rainbow placards de-
manding fairness and equality. Businesses announce that
they welcome gay applicants. Laws prohibit discrimination
on the job and in the military. Public opinion polls show
that Americans stand solidly for marriage equality.

As for me: In 2010, I retired from an extremely satisfying thirty-seven-year career with the Hennepin County
Library system, one of the nation's best. For a while, I
was in charge of training new librarians, so I was able to
influence the way we served the public in every branch
library. When I left, I was a coordinating librarian, one of
the system's top positions. I had the pleasure of overseeing
the design of state-of-the-art libraries that met the specific
needs of each community.

Two years after I retired, and forty-three years after the
Board of Regents rescinded my job offer, University of
Minnesota president Eric Kaler finally issued a public apol-
ogy to me. He said that the university's treatment of me
was "reprehensible" and "regrets that it occurred."

Jack also retired from engineering and law. His last legal battle was in 2002, when he took the IRS to court
over their rejection of our "married, filing jointly" tax re-
turns. With public opinion turning steadily in our favor,
he hoped that he could force the issue into court and speed
up the process of legalizing gay marriage for all. Unfortunately, a medical issue forced him to abandon the lawsuit
before it reached the highest court.

Since our retirement, Jack and I have enjoyed the

time to cultivate this home that we both love. Today, our home bears little resemblance to the worn-out structure that we purchased thirty-four years ago. We re-landscaped our yard. Our woodwork gleams as we walk across oriental rugs. Our walls are graced by the work of local artists, and our dream kitchen is custom-designed to produce the wholesome meals that nurture our bodies.

We began organizing our notes and records to donate them to the Tretter Collection, housed at the University of Minnesota, the same university that played such a large role in our lives. As we searched through years of documents—legal briefs and rulings, posters and photos and letters—I decided that it was time to tell our story in our own words. When the University of Minnesota Press offered to publish this book, we felt that events had come full circle. Jack and I have had a long and complex relationship with this institution. It's where he learned the law. It's where we battled for gay rights. It's where I was denied my job. Now its archive, the Tretter Collection, houses the record of our legal battle for the right to live and love openly. And its press has become the home where our story lives on.

Looking back, I'm proud that Jack and I were the first. Back when we married, gay marriage was a revolutionary idea. Today, marriage equality seems like the most reasonable of notions. Of course gay men and women deserve the right to marry. Legally. Officially. In front of our families and friends, officials and ministers. Of course. Because this is our country.

And yes, in the down-home words of Mother McConnell, we're as good as anybody else.

Epilogue

Two years after marriage equality was achieved in Minnesota, it finally became the law of the land.

On June 26, 2015, the United States Supreme Court ruled in the case known as *Obergefell v. Hodges* that gay couples have a fundamental right to marry. Jack and I rejoiced as we read the long-awaited decision. In their ruling, the justices acknowledged our long struggle. They stated that "*Baker v. Nelson* must be and now is overruled."

The case that spurred the Supreme Court to action had a complicated origin. Unlike our case, which involved one couple attempting to marry, *Obergefell v. Hodges* consolidated six separate cases from four different states. All in all, sixteen same-sex couples, as well as their children and other claimants, were involved.

James Obergefell, the plaintiff whose name graces the ruling, lived in Ohio. Since Ohio did not allow gay marriage, he and John Arthur had married in Maryland. Arthur was terminally ill, and Obergefell wanted to be identified as the surviving spouse on Arthur's death certificate. But for that to happen, Ohio would have to recognize gay marriages that had been performed in another state. Each of the other five cases involved in this landmark decision concerned various issues involving marriage, such as inheritance and custody.

Jack and I had followed gay civil rights struggles for decades, and we knew the Supreme Court ruling was imminent. Over the years, a hodgepodge of court rulings had produced such a tangle of marriage laws that it was time for the Supreme Court to act. Only our country's highest court could end the confusion and give all Americans fair and equal access to the benefits—emotional, economic, and legal—of marriage. After forty-three years, our country's legal system had, at long last, caught up with the simple, logical idea that we proposed when we were young lovers.

Jack and I were both seventy-three years old when we heard the Supreme Court ruling. We had been living quietly in our retirement, basking in the small sunbeams that illuminate the lives of couples like us, couples in steady, loving relationships. We thought our days in court were over. Of course, we had looked forward to the Supreme Court's ruling. It would give thousands of other gay men and women the peace and happiness that we enjoyed. There would be practical considerations as well: with the Supreme Court's decision, we would be able to claim all the economic benefits that marriage confers on straight couples.

Jack and I have always lived modestly, and we have never been in need of basic necessities. For the most part, we've been lucky and enjoyed good health. But we knew that, being older, either one of us might be a mere breath away from a calamity that would strain our resources. Sure, we had savings set aside. But how long would these last if one of us developed a major medical problem? I received more from Social Security than Jack did, and, as my husband, Jack was entitled to receive a portion of my benefits along with his own. That income might become critical to him if I predeceased him. I was entitled to the peace of mind that any family's principal wage-earner deserves: to know that my husband would receive his fair share of the money from my years in the work force.

Anticipating the Supreme Court's ruling on marriage equality, we decided to apply for spousal benefits from Social Security. We would need to present proof of marriage, so in September 2014 I requested official copies of our marriage certificate from Blue Earth County. I received a form from the county's Vital Statistics office with a checked line that stated: "Our office is unable to locate a record as stated in your request." A handwritten note on the form stated: "Marriage records are filed in the county where the license was applied for, in this case it would be Hennepin County."

I knew perfectly well that this was not an innocent mistake on the part of Blue Earth County officials. We had saved a copy of our 1971 marriage certificate, signed by the ordained minister who performed our marriage ceremony. We had a copy of the marriage license that Blue Earth County had issued. We also had the certified mail receipt proving that we had sent our marriage documents to the Blue Earth County's clerk of court. Our marriage has never been revoked or challenged by any court of law. So we knew the county was playing games—pretending that no record of our marriage existed. Pretending they knew nothing about our situation.

In October, we hired an attorney, Dennis J. Dietzler, to request the copies of our marriage records from Blue Earth County. When the county did not comply, he wrote again. With our attorney pressing, Blue Earth County acknowledged that they had a file on our marriage. They sent

Dietzler several documents and letters alleging that since our marriage was invalid, it had never been recorded. In his third request for our marriage record, Dietzler referred to these documents. He wrote: "The letter from the County Attorney mistakes the law as it then existed and failed to justify its conclusion. . . . Because no court ordered Marriage Record No. 22 to be annulled, then or ever, continued refusal to record it will be seen as a deliberate denial of JMM's constitutional right to enjoy equal protection under law."

Although we hadn't received a certified marriage record stamped by Blue Earth County, Jack decided to go ahead and submit his application for spousal benefits. We were eager to get the application submitted as soon as possible because we expected that once the Supreme Court did rule, thousands of gay couples would apply to receive spousal benefits, and there would be a significant backlog. Jack presented a signed copy of our marriage certificate to the Social Security office on December 22, 2015. We hoped this "proof" would be sufficient, and we could bypass any further dealings with the stubborn officials of Blue Earth County.

On February 2, 2015, our attorney received a letter from Mark A. Lindahl, Blue Earth County's Assistant County Attorney. It concluded: "Because the Blue Earth County Attorney's Office determined that the marriage license issued on August 31, 1971, was legally defective and that a lawful marriage did not arise from that license, the marriage was not considered valid and has not been recorded. We cannot, therefore, provide you with certified copies of the marriage record."

When I read that letter, I could feel my blood begin to boil. Here was the age-old bully who lurked in the shadows, waiting to pounce on gay men and women. In spite of the fact that polls showed that public opinion had shifted and a majority of Americans now believed that gay men and women had the right to marry, the fossilized officials in Blue Earth County refused to budge. Good grief! What did they have to gain by refusing to record our marriage? My civil rights were being violated—just as they were when the University of Minnesota's Board of Regents rescinded my job offer in 1970. I told Jack that if they insisted on fighting it out in court, I was ready.

"Are you sure that's what you want, Michael? You remember how long a lawsuit takes? There'll be months of motions, appeals, hearings." He shrugged. "If we don't get spousal benefits, so what? We'll make do with what we have."

I scowled. It wasn't like Jack to urge moderation. But I understood his reluctance. Neither of us were spring colts. Did we still have the energy to kick down gates and jump over fences?

Jack kept checking back with a Social Security agent every month or two to inquire about the status of his request for spousal benefits. After several months, it was clear that Social Security would not grant his request until Blue Earth County provided a certified record of our marriage. This meant that we would either need to mount a lawsuit against the county or we would have to relinquish our right to spousal benefits.

I've never been good at giving up. And the thought

of caving into a bully was eating away at me. One night at dinner, I served up an announcement along with our food. "I want to do it," I told Jack.

Jack raised his eyebrows and gave me a mischievous grin. "Here I thought we were too old to ignore dinner and jump into bed. But, Michael, if that's what you want . . ."

I rolled my eyes. "You know perfectly well what I'm talking about. And it's not a romp between the sheets. The Supreme Court ruled that we have the right to marry. We're entitled to spousal benefits from Social Security. Why should we let Blue Earth County rob us? Why let them bully us out of our constitutional rights? If they want to fight, let's go for it. I say we hire a law firm and sue the pants off Blue Earth County."

Jack nodded. "If that's what you want, that's what we'll do. But don't go expecting a quick answer in court. You know how long these things take."

I looked at my husband. One slim arm was propped on the table, and white hair fell softly about his ears. He looked tired. He's as handsome in my eyes as the young man I met nearly half a century ago at a dance in Oklahoma. But in the eyes of the world, Jack looks like an older man. Sure, he's still nimble enough to scurry up and down our stairs, carry in the groceries, and shovel the walk. But how long will that last? Let's face it—he's no longer the strong, forceful guy who marched in the struggle for gay rights. Neither am I. Was it a good idea to charge into another legal battle? How much would this cost us—both in dollars and effort? Maybe we belonged on the sidelines now. Maybe we should accept that we're two old horses, strong enough to pad around the pasture and that's about it.

Jack turned to me and winked. An adorable grin erased his wrinkles, and his eyes began to dance with mischief. "You know, I didn't want to force you into anything, Michael. But I think this lawsuit is a good idea. And long overdue. As a matter of fact, I wondered how long it was going to take you to decide to do it."

And that is how we entered our final court battle. Inspired by the Supreme Court's declaration that marriage is a fundamental right of every American, we decided to sue Blue Earth County for denying our constitutional rights. We were going to demand complete equality—no apologies, no excuses.

We contacted the Fredrikson & Byron law firm of Minneapolis, the second largest law firm in Minnesota. On April 1, 2016, they offered to take our case. Cynthia A. Moyer would be our lead attorney. We liked her immediately. She radiated confidence as well as competence, plus she had a terrific smile. She told us that since our case involved civil rights and had historic implications, the firm offered to waive their attorneys' fees. Our case would be part of the pro bono work that they supply as a service to the community, and we would pay only incidentals, like filing and duplicating costs. (But if Blue Earth County lost, they would be required to pay all the court costs, including fees for our attorneys.) Working with Moyer would be attorney Richard D. Snyder as the litigator, as well as attorneys Anu Sreekanth and Kristy Dahl Rogers.

Our case was named *James Michael McConnell et al. vs.*

Blue Earth County et al. or, for ease of reference, McConnells against Blue Earth County. We delivered all the documents concerning our marriage to Moyer. She and her team were optimistic about the outcome and expected a quick judgment in our favor when we appeared in District Court, Fifth Judicial District. Our hearing was set for January 12, 2017.

At the hearing, our attorneys presented our case to a judge. (This was not the sort of case that involves a jury.) Snyder argued that our marriage had never been dissolved or annulled in any court. No grounds existed to invalidate the marriage. Therefore, we were requesting a writ of mandamus, an order for Blue Earth County to comply with their legal duty to record our marriage.

Blue Earth County hired a Mankato law firm, and their attorney defended the county's actions by accusing us of fraud because neither of us was a permanent citizen of the county when we applied for our marriage license. Our attorneys argued that this was a silly defense because Mankato is a college town and many temporary residents apply for marriage licenses; the residency requirement was generally ignored. And, our attorneys pointed out, fraud would actually be an irrelevant defense: in 1953, the state supreme court had ruled that even if a marriage license was based on fraud, the marriage stands so long as the marriage contract was validated. Only a judge has the power to dissolve a validated marriage.

The county also tried to defend itself by complaining that the clerk had assumed that our marriage was between a man and a woman. But no requirement specifying gender had existed in the state's statutes.

It took ninety days for the judge to rule, and our legal team seemed as disappointed with his decision as we were. The judge acknowledged that our claims were valid. But in a district court, a judge has the "discretion" to offer an alternative course of action rather than granting the plaintiff's demands. The judge declined to grant a writ of mandamus. He spared the county officials the humiliation resulting from an order that implied they had not done their legal duty. Instead the judge offered his solution: that we get married again, either in Blue Earth County or anyplace else.

"What a ridiculous ruling!" Jack declared as soon as we read the decision. "We're already married. A judge is advising us to commit bigamy. He's telling us to break the law. This is the stupidest ruling I've ever heard."

Of course there were other reasons why marrying again would not be a fair solution. Practical reasons, like fulfilling length-of-marriage requirements for Social Security benefits. And emotional reasons: we did not want to erase our reputation as the world's first legally married gay couple, which is a source of enormous pride and satisfaction for us. We spearheaded a movement that reverberated around the planet, and we deserve to be remembered as the pioneers of marriage equality. There's no way that we would undo our title of "first," a title that had cost us so much.

Our legal team advised us to appeal, so we began preparations. The appellate court hearing took place on September 28, 2017. Another disappointment. The judges ruled 2 to 1 against us. They said we had not presented sufficient evidence to support our claim.

The next step was the Minnesota State Supreme Court. It denied our petition for a hearing because our case did not affect a large group of citizens of the state. This was not a ruling. Instead, the court declined to hear our case because the outcome would have relevancy for only two individuals: this was a court's way of saying that ours was not the type of case that should be decided in a higher court. In this situation, a case is automatically sent back to the first court (the Fifth Judicial District Court) for a ruling.

The next hearing was our last chance, and our legal team beefed up the evidence so our case would not be denied for want of information. All the principal parties were deposed, which means that we were interviewed by an attorney from the opposing side, and our testimony was recorded for the judge to read. During the depositions, which took place at the law firm representing Blue Earth County, our attorneys interviewed the assistant clerk of court who issued our marriage license and her boss, the clerk of court. Both of these women are now grandmothers, and they explained, as best they remembered, what happened in the county's office forty-six years ago in 1971 when they issued our marriage license and when the office received our marriage certificate in the mail. Jack and I were both interviewed by an attorney for Blue Earth County.

Another part of the preparation for the hearing is called "discovery." That's when various documents and other evidence are shown to the opposing side. When our legal team examined Marriage Record No. 22 submitted by Blue Earth County, we discovered a shocking piece of deceit. When our previous attorney had requested our records, Blue Earth County had submitted a falsified copy of our application for marriage. They had covered up the bottom lines of the original document. This time, we saw the complete document, which contained a handwritten note: "Rated Defective by County Attorney—8-31-71—Notices Mailed Cert Mail to both parties."

As soon as we saw that note, we realized that Blue Earth County had probably lost their case. A county attorney did not have the authority to declare a marriage "defective"—that requires a court decision. This was a flagrant abuse of power. Worse still, the county had concealed the note when it sent a copy to our previous attorney. That amounts to lying.

Our final hearing was on September 17, 2018, in the Blue Earth County Courthouse in Mankato, with Assistant Chief Judge Gregory Anderson presiding. Jack and I were optimistic that we would get a ruling in our favor, so I wasn't scared during the hour and a half drive from Minneapolis. But I can't say I was totally confident, either. We've been through enough trials to know that outcomes can surprise. Even flabbergast.

The courthouse was a standard government building, beige and wood, comfortable enough but without any frills. We sat on benches that resembled pews in a church. Roger Lynn, the United Methodist minister who married us in 1971, has remained our friend through all these years. (He's always maintained that we were his most successful marriage, since Jack and I have been a loving couple for almost half a century.) We had invited him to join us in court. Generous and supportive as always, Roger and his wife agreed to make an eight-hour drive to Mankato. Ten other friends also attended the hearing. On our side of the courtroom, Jack and I were surrounded by twelve of our friends and three of our attorneys.

The opposing side, representing Blue Earth County, was practically deserted—only one attorney attended the hearing.

The hearing lasted twenty or thirty minutes. Sitting there, I felt like I was having an out-of-body experience. We were at the end of the road. After forty-seven years of struggles and setbacks, we were about to hear a judge speak the words that we had fought a lifetime to hear.

And that's exactly what he did. Judge Anderson's statement was straightforward, and he delivered it in a clear voice. He declared: "The September 3, 1971, marriage of James Michael McConnell and Pat Lyn McConnell, a/k/a Richard John Baker, has never been dissolved or annulled by judicial decree and no grounds currently exist on which to invalidate the marriage. The marriage is declared to be in all respects valid."

When he finished speaking, our friends applauded. Although applause is considered inappropriate in a courtroom, Judge Anderson flashed a teeny smile. On the benches around us, the smiles were titanic. Our friends grabbed each other and hugged. Tears of joy moistened eyes and threatened mascara. Our attorneys beamed. Unsure if my legs would support me, I reached for Jack as we filed out of the courtroom. Yes, we expected this outcome. Definitely, we deserved this outcome. But words can't convey the emotion that flooded me. Imagine the stupendous joy of it—nearly half a century after we pledged to love and honor each other for the rest of our lives, Jack and I were officially husband and husband. We proved it. We proved we have the right to love and wed in the sunlight.

When we returned to Minneapolis that afternoon, dozens of congratulations scrolled across my Facebook page. Among them were these words from Minnesota state senator Scott Dibble: "Today is an enormously historic day. At long last, by order of the court, Minnesota's Michael McConnell and Jack Baker, who in 1971 became the first same sex couple in the U.S., and the world, to apply for a marriage license and marry have had that marriage fully and legally validated. My husband, Richard Leyva, and I were honored to be in the presence of these two courageous heroes! Congratulations, Michael and Jack. Thank you for forging the way!!"

Our journey was nearly finished, but there was one step left: a decision from the Social Security Administration. Now we would be dealing not with a court but with a bureaucracy. After our triumph in court, we were primed to leap across the finish line. But if there's anything slower than a court, it's a bureaucracy.

On October 6, 2018, Jack sent a letter and supporting documents by certified mail to the Social Security Administration. Then we waited. And waited. And waited some more. When we had not heard by the end of the year, we decided to ask for help. We wrote to U.S. Senator Amy Klobuchar on January 30, 2019.

On February 12, Klobuchar's office called to notify Jack that his Social Security claim had been approved. On February 16, the Social Security Administration sent the official letter: "We are writing to let you know that you are entitled to monthly husband benefits on the record of James McConnell's beginning June 2015."

Since the Social Security Administration is an arm of our federal government, that simple, routine notice confirmed a momentous fact: we are the first legally recognized same-sex marriage in the world.

I've always believed that love is the most powerful force in the universe. At last, at the age of seventy-six, Jack and I proved it.

Acknowledgments

Many people added their love to our love story. In particular, I thank my parents, J.D. and Vera McConnell, for their unconditional acceptance of me as well as Jack, whom they called "our other son." Over the decades, we have appreciated the caring support of my little sister Sherre Giezentanner and her husband, Brent; my big brother Jerry McConnell and his wife, Carroll; and my big sisters Betty Nettleton and Pat Williams. Although I never had the joy of meeting Jack's grandmother Margaret Danek, who died while he was on active duty in the U.S. Air Force, I know she was the bedrock of his childhood. Jack's favorite sister, Judé Loferski, and her husband, Gene, have meant the world to us over the years. Today our lives are richer for our nieces, nephews, and cousins.

Jack and I met almost fifty years ago. Many friends have sustained us during these years, starting with the members of FREE, the University of Minnesota student group that sponsored our marriage. Two people deserve special mention: the courageous Reverend Roger Lynn, the Methodist minister who married us and so transformed our lives, and Terry Vanderplas, who created our golden wedding rings, which are still strong and beautiful, tangible symbols of our commitment.

Our life's story grew from the help and encouragement of many people. The Hennepin County Library System gave me an amazing thirty-seven-year career. During that time, dozens of colleagues became enduring friends. Lisa Vecoli, the wonderful curator of the Jean-Nickolaus

Tretter Collection of the University of Minnesota Libraries, helped us preserve the records of our journey.

The University of Minnesota Press contributed far more than we could have hoped from a publisher. In addition to professional guidance, our editor, Erik Anderson, as well as his assistant, Kristian Tvedten, the folks in the marketing department, especially Emily Hamilton and Heather Skinner, and director Doug Armato delight us with their enthusiasm, expertise, and insight.

Completing the dream team that made this book possible is our writer, Gail Langer Karwoski. We have known her since the early seventies, and when we set out to tell our story, we knew that she was the only person who could translate the complex records of our lives into an accurate and compelling memoir. During the years we have worked on this project, she has managed to speak our hearts in my voice. Our gratitude also extends to her husband, Chester, who never wavered in his encouragement—no matter how many trips she took to our home, no matter how much time she lavished on this book.

Index

Michael McConnell and Jack Baker are America's first legally married gay couple. They were married in Minneapolis in September 1971 in a small ceremony officiated by a Methodist minister, with an official license issued by a rural Minnesota county. They met in 1966 in Norman, Oklahoma. In 2010, Michael retired from the Hennepin County Library System and Jack retired from his careers in law and engineering. They live in Minneapolis.

Gail Langer Karwoski is an author and educator based in Athens, Georgia. She met Michael McConnell and Jack Baker in 1972, the year after they were married.